LETTERS TO LALAGE

Letters to Lalage

THE LETTERS OF CHARLES WILLIAMS
TO LOIS LANG-SIMS

with commentary by Lois Lang-Sims
introduction and notes by Glen Cavaliero

THE KENT STATE UNIVERSITY PRESS
Kent, Ohio, and London, England

© 1989 by The Kent State University Press, Kent, Ohio 44242
All rights reserved
Library of Congress Catalog Card Number 89-33241
ISBN 0-87338-398-2
Manufactured in the United States of America

The originals of the Lois Lang-Sims letters are part of the Marion E. Wade Center, Wheaton College, Wheaton, Illinois, USA. Researchers may consult them there.

Library of Congress Cataloging-in-Publication Data

Williams, Charles, 1886–1945.
    Letters to Lalage : the letters of Charles Williams to Lois Lang-Sims / with commentary by Lois Lang-Sims ; introduction and notes by Glen Cavaliero.
        p.   cm.
    ISBN 0-87338-398-2 (alk. paper ∞)
    1. Williams, Charles, 1886–1945—Correspondence.   2. Authors, English—20th century—Correspondence.   3. Lang-Sims, Lois—Correspondence.   I. Lang-Sims, Lois.   II. Cavaliero, Glen, 1927–
III. Title.
PR6045.I5Z487   1989
828'.91209—dc20
[B]   89-33241
                                                                                                    CIP

British Library Cataloguing-in-Publication data are available.

To Joan Wallis
in memory of Charles
and in gratitude for
forty years of mutual
affection and respect

Contents

Introduction   1
The Letters with Commentary   15
Notes   87

A Note on the Text

Charles Williams used some unusual punctuation in his letters. The marks ". ." and ". . ." are reproduced as they appear in the original letters and do not represent any omission from the text. Quotation marks are reproduced as used in the originals as well.

Introduction

The short-lived but remarkable correspondence presented in the following pages took place toward the end of Charles Williams' life. He was at this time lodging in Oxford, where the London branch of the University Press had taken up residence on the outbreak of the Second World War. He acted for them as an editor and literary adviser, and it was the first time he had worked outside the capital city which had provided him with so much inspiration. Williams was a man of exceptional intellectual energy, for in addition to his work at the Press and as a teacher of evening classes in English literature he was a prolific author. By the time these letters were written he had published over thirty books in a number of different fields.

Lois Lang-Sims was not the first young woman to seek his help or to fall beneath his spell. When she wrote to him in September 1943 Williams already had numerous admirers, pupils, and disciples who looked to him for counsel, for advice and, most especially, for encouragement. He possessed enormous personal magnetism, not least because his appearance and behaviour could be strange and disconcerting. But this power to attract people was balanced by a sharp, incisive intellect, the rhapsodic utterance of his lectures and personal correspondence being matched by a consistency of thought that was embodied in his novels, poems, plays, biographies, and books of literary criticism and theology. Above all, his personal and professional activities were informed by a profound awareness of the metaphysical dimension in which they had their being.

In this respect his affinity with Lois Lang-Sims was not surprising. Some thirty years younger than he was, she was in due course herself to become a forceful and individual writer whose literary output, though relatively small, was almost as varied as Williams' own. Her novel, *The Contrite Heart* (1968), has a hallucinatory, haunting quality; it takes the form of a nineteenth-century English pastoral, with a piercing sense of good and evil reminiscent in places of the novels of another writer with an unfashionable consciousness of unseen forces, Phyllis Paul. In a different genre, the descriptive history *Canterbury Cathedral* (1979) is, like Williams' *The Descent of the Dove*, as much concerned with the metaphysical dimension of its subject matter as with chronological progression. Her first book, *The Presence of Tibet* (1963), is a plea for that country's religious culture in the context of its takeover by the forces of Communist China; while *A Time to be Born* (1971) and *Flower in a Teacup* (1973) are searching exercises in self-analytical autobiography, the former containing a brief but trenchant account of the author's friendship with Charles Williams. Still more indebted to him is her exposition of esoteric Christianity, *The Christian Mystery* (1980). This is a book so alien to contemporary theological fashion as to have slipped out of sight almost unnoticed; yet it remains one which any admirer of Williams would find congenial, for it definitively refutes the literal-mindedness against which he himself so frequently protested. In Lois Lang-Sims' writings, as in those of Charles Williams, a variety of literary forms embody a singleness of imaginative vision. But at the time of their first meeting she was only twenty-six years old and, according to *A Time to be Born*, in a state of great mental and emotional confusion. Now, nearly fifty years later, she presents the letters Williams wrote to her, together with her own comments on a relationship that was to come to such an abrupt, and in some respects disturbing, end.

His friends and associates knew Charles Williams in a variety of capacities and roles. Those who shared in his membership of the Fellowship of the Rosy Cross, or in his home life in Hampstead, or in his work at Amen House, or in the various Institutes of Higher Education at which he taught his evening classes, would each see different aspects of him; but for the most part each would remain in that particular circle. The intense demands of Williams' mental and imaginative life did not permit him to be readily or relaxedly gregarious, though in whatever company he happened to be, for example as part of the Inklings group at Oxford, he was a powerful presence. But these *Letters to Lalage* enable us to study his involvement in one particular relationship with one particular person. As such they form an invaluable supplement to the more general accounts of Williams' life supplied by his biographers. The letters also demonstrate the facility, if not in every case the aptitude, with which he could express himself in verse.

As Lois Lang-Sims points out, it is impossible to separate Charles Williams' character and personality from his published work; indeed, one might almost say that it is impossible to distinguish them. Certainly as a writer Williams blends to a remarkable degree those seemingly contradictory characteristics of impersonality and mannered idiosyncracy which were a feature of his daily bearing. More than in the case of most authors, one's reaction to his ideas and their presentation is bound up with one's reaction to his personality; and the story contained in this correspondence recounts one such response and its effect upon the object of it. We see here something of the hypnotic quality of Charles Williams' character and may obtain from it a deep if glancing insight into his extremely vulnerable humanity. At times a painful document, *Letters to Lalage* is of the greatest value in illuminating some of the more troubled aspects of a Christian writer and teacher who, more convincingly than most, could evoke the nature of joy— and who could induce joy in other people, however precariously he may have been aware of it himself. Most especially this book gives one an insight into the price Charles Williams paid (and unwittingly exacted) for his particular gifts and vision.

The outer events of his life have already been recorded in three biographies, two of them by his colleague and close friend, Alice Mary Hadfield, whose loving accounts of Williams' teaching and personality describe the positive aspects of his effect upon those who knew him well. Humphrey Carpenter's *The Inklings* (1978) is more detached, focusing on Williams' Oxford years and his friendship with C. S. Lewis. But from both these books one is made aware not only of his powerful influence upon most of the people with whom he came in contact, but also of the rather precarious social foundations on which his career was built. Shortage of money was to harass him all his days. He did not come from the well-to-do, public-school-educated middle-class to which the majority of his literary contemporaries belonged. His father was a clerk working for a firm in the City of London; later he and his wife ran a small stationer's shop in the cathedral town of St. Albans. Williams grew up in a pious, self-enclosed family world, which a close imaginative relationship with his father only served to make the more sufficient. Both of his biographers record the existence of a lively, ongoing fantasy life, the creation of imaginary courts and ceremonies and countries such as one finds in the childhood and youth of many other writers—the Brontë sisters, for instance, or Arthur Ransome and E. R. Eddison, Christopher Isherwood and Edward Upward, J. R. R. Tolkien and C. S. Lewis, to name a few. In the cases of Eddison and Tolkien this preoccupation resulted in objectively realised literary re-creations; in that of Charles Williams not only did his fantasy world issue in poetry and fiction, it was also imposed upon the circumstances of his daily life and in due course even upon the people who shared in them. He thus sought to combine the roles of both poet and magician through the projection and acting out of an intellectual and imaginative myth.

This myth, to which reference is repeatedly made in the following pages, is that of King Arthur and the Holy Grail—as Williams came to interpret it. His intellectual conclusions, together with their scholarly foundation, can be found in the unfinished "The Figure of Arthur" and in a number of the essays and reviews that were collected after his death by Anne Ridler in *The Image of the City* (1958). They provide a key to the meaning of the otherwise obscure and baffling (though always colourful and impressive) poems in *Taliessin Through Logres* (1938) and *The Region of the Summer Stars* (1944). But these poems were the public articulation of a more purely personal concern, which the various strands and symbols of the myth were to embody in an elaborate web of metaphor.

As Lois Lang-Sims was to discover to her cost, Williams' identification of himself with Taliessin, the King's poet, was more total than he himself was perhaps aware. The inmost experiences of his outwardly uneventful life made this entirely natural. He was involved for over ten years in the study of occult and cabbalistic lore and of its corresponding rituals: for him the wisdom of alchemy and magic, disowned by twentieth-century scientific materialism, had provided a viable method of interpreting the spiritual laws of the universe, and, indeed, of expounding the doctrines of Christianity. This Hermetic interpretation of the Faith, although subsumed into the more orthodox vision of his later years, nonetheless gives to his religious writings an impression of stasis, a stress upon pattern rather than on process, on eternity rather than on time. The universe is read and understood rather as though it were a poem—for Williams, as though it were an Arthurian poem. Everything is related to everything else as part of one created whole. His imagination was obsessed by the concept of organic structure.

The locating and particularising of this sense of structure in his work at the Oxford University Press was psychologically the response to his otherwise constricted circumstances—a constriction, however, that was to some extent of his own choosing. It suited his temperament to live by the routine and in the particular places that he did. He needed a life with limitations in order to support the myth, and he fed his own experience of fellowship and sharing into the master pattern, treating the Press's Editor-in-chief, Sir Humphrey Milford, as though he were Imperial Caesar, and interpreting his own work and that of his colleagues as metaphorical enactments of divinely appointed laws. The expression of this vision in his poetry was to become the chief literary preoccupation of his life; and it is open to question whether it did not in due course amount to an obsession. Certainly, as the *Letters to Lalage* suggest, there was some danger of the symbolic expression of the materially apprehended reality being imposed back upon that reality. That this should be the case was the result of the myth itself being the clothing not only of an intellectual system but also of a psychological need.

That need was real enough. The factual basis of the tragic predicament in Williams' personal life, at which he hints in one of these letters, has been described by his biographers. His transference to another woman of the romantic adoration he had bestowed upon his wife was, to a man of his deep Christian convictions and with his sense of an inexorable moral and spiritual pattern, almost literally an "impossible" situation; while the subsequent transference of his second love's affection to one of his friends and colleagues tightened the contradiction further still. That Williams bore the cruel situation without breaking down may in part be attributed to the fact that he had the mythology to resort to; he could externalise and dramatise the inner pain just as he externalised and dramatised the world of his employment and his marriage. His wife was renamed by him "Michal"; his second love became "Phillida," then "Celia": they were to that slight extent already held a little distant from him. It was perhaps because of this that he was able to maintain his relationship with each of the two women; but the cost to himself was devastating. By the time he met Lois Lang-Sims the myth was the master-pattern of his life.

By 1933 Williams' supplanter, Gerard Hopkins, was detached enough to dramatise their story in a novel with the astringent title of *Nor Fish Nor Flesh*. Williams himself was spurred into still greater mental and literary activity: the early thirties were to be his most productive years, despite the strain in which he lived. That strain was not only the result of divided loyalties and frustrated passion: it was inherent in the kind of man Charles Williams was. The tremendous nervous energy and concentrated force of intellect which lies behind his literary output may well have demanded a wider personal outlet than the devotion of his evening classes was able to afford. His own awareness of the lure of power, in his case of spiritual power, was keen; he dallies with that lure in his first novel, *Shadows of Ecstasy*, with its ambiguous portrayal of Nigel Considine; and rejects it in the portrayal of Clerk Simon in his last one, *All Hallows' Eve*. But it remains likely that he underwent a good deal of suppressed frustration on the purely material level of his life. The failure, for financial reasons, to complete his degree course at London University must surely have rankled a little. His ability was in excess of his opportunities, at any rate in his earlier years; it seems likely that his engagement in occult studies and, later, in spiritual direction, were to some extent substitutes for the more secular outlets which his social and financial circumstances denied him.

Where the occult studies are concerned, Williams was more deeply involved than his friends and commentators were aware. His membership of the Fellowship of the Rosy Cross lasted for at least eleven years; and although, as R. A. Gilbert points out, the Order "was always his servant, never his master," it did minister to his tendency to subordinate individual personalities to the requirements of mythology. The transformation of the young woman Lois into the slave girl Lalage is a case in point, and one cannot but interpret the clear-eyed challenge she threw back at him as constituting the dispersal of mist and the breaking of a spell, evidence to the master himself that truth did not inhere in any material order subject to laws that were predictable and which could therefore be controlled. Intellectually Williams did not need to be told this; but psychologically it would seem that he did.

The situation was poignant rather than sinister. Lois Lang-Sims' suggestion that Williams was incapable of human relationships at any deep personal level, while refuted by the devotion of his pupils, friends, and colleagues, contains a modicum of truth where the term 'relationship' is concerned. His early poems are full of a sense of stark interior loneliness, while the very self-consciousness with which he writes of love and marriage suggests that he did not take readily to the latter state. But the poems are no less remarkable for their demonstration that Williams himself was aware that this was the case: in domestic matters his overpowering belief in a transcendent mystery may have proved embarrassing. Certainly the letters to his wife which have survived tend to be written in the same courtly, mannered idiom in which he addressed his other female correspondents.

Lois Lang-Sims is probably right in declaring that Michal Williams had a character as unusual as that of her husband. My own friendship with her, which lasted from 1954 until her death in 1970, was always affectionate and serene, though I soon realised that there were certain areas into which it was perilous to trespass. One of these was the way in which, so she felt, the guardianship of her husband's literary reputation had been stolen from her by certain of his friends, especially those at the Press: she could be both sorrowful and devastatingly caustic on that topic. That she was sympathetic to Williams' literary work and shared in its composition, her brief memoir "As I Remember" makes amply clear; and she had a warm regard for Dorothy L. Sayers, Anne Ridler, and "my beloved Jack Lewis," none of whom she associated with her husband's relationship with "Celia." And she could be extremely funny about the earnest research students who sought her out in connection with their theses on Williams' writings. But while sceptical concerning his activities as spiritual counsellor, she was prepared on occasion to make use of his mythological vocabulary. Her own rather regal bearing and beautiful dark eyes enhanced the effect of this; but the majestic manner was qualified by a nervous tenseness, an impulsive eagerness of response which made her seem extremely vulnerable. Her attitude to her husband could vary almost painfully. She would refer to him as "ineffable" and "endearing" and speak of "all that was so shining and lovely in his morning time," and in connection with his biographers and literary executor, "I could cry 'They have taken away my lord.' " But when stung into bitter recollections by the publication of some reference, however delicate, to his other love, she could write that in marrying Charles Williams she had married a cross; and she was withering about those whom she regarded as being predatory, his women friends and disciples especially, and the "chew-string gaseous" colloquies in which, according to her, they so greedily indulged. I think she would have disliked her husband's correspondence with "Lalage," and have applauded the latter's determination to resume her own identity. Even so, as Lois Lang-Sims suggests, her friendship with anyone related to him in this way was at best sporadic.

The nature of Charles Williams' relationship with his disciples (the word is inescapable) is of course one of the critical questions raised by these letters and their accompanying effects. In this regard it is worth pointing out that any relationship is determined by the natures of both parties, and that Williams' dealings with other young women will probably have been of a somewhat different character: indeed, there is enough evidence in the biographies to suggest that this was so. That he sensed in this particular disciple an independence of judgement and a forthright truthfulness that would be anything but adulatory is evident from the convoluted and often self-protective nature of his letters. Moreover, those qualities could themselves by their very nature have evoked the threats, and both the acts, of corporal punishment.

It seems likely that the punishments were obliquely masochistic: whatever else, as their recipient points out, they were not consonant with a fully adult relationship. By this time in his life Williams was clearly living in the extremity of nervous tension, and the letters show it. Some of them are so elliptical and allusive as to be well-nigh unintelligible, reading more like the words of a man in colloquy with himself than those of one engaged in dialogue with another. He would in any case have sensed his correspondent's feelings towards him, and have been manoeuvering behind a smoke-screen, deploying that strategy of oblique self-distancing which anyone endowed with eloquence and personal magnetism has to learn to exercise. But the endless shifting qualifications and paradoxes were not there simply in order that he might protect himself. They are manifestations of his abiding awareness that the positing of any particular truth must of necessity be relative.

Williams' own depression and sceptical nature had been saved from despair by a kind of counter-scepticism which he called "defeated irony." If nothing was certain then everything was possible—even hope. His early writings, especially the poems in *Windows of Night* (1925) and the books written at the onset of his personal crisis with regard to "Celia," had invoked what he called in one poem "The Angel of Intellectual Doubt" or "The Protector," who was the guardian of faith against superstition, hypocrisy, and despair. And when Williams came to be the focus of that group of people whom he christened "The Companions of the Co-Inherence" it was this "doubt of all things seen" which alerted him to the spiritual dangers of his position. It also became the foundation of his own theology and spiritual perspective.

Throughout Williams' work one is constantly made aware of the dictum (its source remains a matter of dispute) "This also is Thou: neither is this Thou." He quoted it continually. It defines the distinction between immanence and transcendence. God as the source and informing spirit of life in all its forms (what Williams liked to call "the derivations") is to be encountered in all experience, though the nature of that encounter is dictated by human freedom, itself a manifestation of Divine activity. There is nothing of which it cannot be said "This also is Thou"—Williams was categorical about this; but at the same time God of His very nature remains unknowable, utterly other, not to be equated with His manifestations— "Neither is this Thou." For Williams, this doctrine was a safeguard against the tendency of religious people to become protective towards the Godhead; it was also the theological basis for tolerance and intellectual humility, and for, in his own phrase, "the beautiful grace of thinking one may be mistaken."

This emphasis on the necessarily relative nature of religious knowledge may also be attributed to Williams' withdrawal from occult studies and to his discovery in the early 1930s of the work of Søren Kierkegaard. The latter's distinction between the spheres of the aesthetic, the ethical, and the religious are relevant to Williams' own spiritual progress. The first sphere is the experience of natural religion, the perception of harmony between the inner life of the soul and the ongoing life of the senses. To this harmony the ethical absolutes constitute a contradiction and a threat. The conflict between the two experiences was described by Williams as "The Impossibility," a state which might be defined as the experience in pain of the paradox "This also is Thou: neither is this Thou." It is what he elsewhere calls "the alteration in knowledge," and he refers to it more than once in the following letters; it is the coincidence of the "is" and the "is not." But beyond it lies the religious sphere in which the paradox is accepted and known as an occasion of joy. Williams attempts to depict such rapture in his novels, most notably in the spiritual experiences of the Archdeacon in *War in Heaven* and of Sybil in *The Greater Trumps;* but in his own life, most particularly in the Celian experience, he apprehended the joy in a state of painful tension.

His own myth, of which the following pages give such a graphic picture, may have been, as I have suggested, as much self-protective as instinctive. The game, so to call it, found its natural expression in allocated names and roles: that way there could be no misleading confusion between image and reality. The truth of "Neither is this Thou" is the more obvious the more blatantly artificial an image is. By assigning to himself the role of Taliessin and by elevating his friends into a Company, Williams could simultaneously assert the relativity of his position as spiritual leader and director, and secure himself from the personal involvement which he was emotionally ill-equipped to undergo. For him, the ceremoniousness, the mythological vocabulary, the endlessly circling paradoxes served as the walls of a fort. But as his friendship with Lois Lang-Sims reveals, this could be a matter of intense pain to the other party concerned, and indicates an essential limitation in the stance of resolute, dispassionate balance. It could in itself become an absolute, and thus an idol.

Williams was, of course, perfectly aware of this. For all his addiction to logical, diagrammatic thinking, his (in Kierkegaardian terms) essentially aesthetic presentation of theology, he knew that so far as Christianity was concerned there was one image of God which could be endorsed without reservation—the historic personage of Jesus of Nazareth (though even here "Neither is this Thou" would seem to be enforced by Christ Himself, in his direction of His disciples' attention away from Himself towards the Father). God is to be found in the muddle, confusion, and commitments of the ordinary, of flesh and blood, in what Yeats calls "the fury and the mire of human veins." And it was, so it would seem, in this sphere that Williams underwent his own defeat. His self-consciousness, his well-nigh crippling rapidity of intellect, his craving for order and his adoration of design, were at a loss in the gross confusion of humankind's incorrigible capacity for passion. It is a characteristic limitation in many intellectuals, and where Williams' relationship with this particular disciple was concerned she was surely right in feeling that it was "Lalage" he wanted, not the real Lois.

This contention brings one up against the peculiar nature of Williams' direction of souls, an avocation normally reserved for the ordained clergy. The concept of the spiritual life in the Catholic tradition rests on the assumption that to find its identity the soul has to do so through discovering its vocation in the mind of its Creator, Who not only confers that identity but shapes it out of circumstances in accordance with that Will to which the soul learns to conform. The soul (meaning here the total human being, body and spirit) is thus both glorious on account of its identity and original nature, and imperfect with respect to its opposition to its destiny. In terms of Williams' mythological language, Lois has to become Lalage the slave girl, who is in her turn the type of Dindrane (or Celia) who is destined to become Beatrice and thus the mother of Love. But why *slave* girl? As a figure of "the old man on the new way" (to use Williams' own phrase from *He Came Down From Heaven*) and thus a slave to the passions, the figure will serve; metaphorically, a slave *boy* would do as well. But in view of Williams' own fascination with the images and the practise of power, one can see a personal compulsion fulfilling itself as well. Theologically, the slave girl embodies a necessary stage of growth, for in the mind of God Lois is identical with Lalage and her successive fulfillments; but in the life of time and of fallen humanity the roles fail to coincide. Williams' spiritual direction of souls was designed to clarify their relative functions, and it consisted for the most part in adjusting attitudes and in maintaining balance between a seriousness which would not degenerate into a self-indulgent introspection, and a joyous freedom which would not relapse into a slothful sensuality. What was unusual about his counselling was that he treated it as being in its turn something relative, as an image, a dance, a game. Hence the oscillation in his letters between playfulness and dedication; hence the uncertainty of tone where he himself is concerned, the capitalised "We," the resort to hierarchical values, all of which seem to distance and de-personalise his role. One is reminded of the Catholic distinction between the ordained priesthood and the man who ministers it, a distinction as necessary to the sanity of the priest himself as the Liturgy's formal ceremonial is necessary for the deliverance of its participants from self-awareness—a function, as Williams himself observed, of all ceremonial, whether secular or religious.

As to the personal style of Williams' counselling, Lois Lang-Sims herself says what is necessary in this particular instance. But before considering the curious sexual overtones of his resort to corporal punishment (an aspect of the affair repellant to customary religious and moral sensibility) it is worth pointing out that this kind of religious direction and counselling inevitably involves a sexual factor where men and women are concerned, which expresses itself in a strictly regulated role-playing. Williams' own penchant for dramatisation may, however, have made him ill at ease in such a predetermined part; and the uncertainty is evident in these letters. Where the "Father" image is eschewed, complications inevitably arise.

The uncertainty may also in part account for the stress on, and the infliction of, specific punishments. Lois Lang-Sims' interpretation of the matter as being an instance of Williams' interest in the arousal and redirection of unsatisfied desire is to some extent supported by his writings, *Shadows of Ecstasy* in particular; and it is more than likely that he would have come across esoteric sexual teaching in the course of his occult studies. As Lois Lang-Sims observes, such practices are familiar to Hindu and Buddhist Tantric adepts. But in any case Williams was not alone in his concern with the subject. A distinguished contemporary, John Cowper Powys, likewise a novelist, poet, philosopher, and critic, though very different in temperament and outlook (where religion was concerned he was a complete agnostic) nonetheless shared with Williams certain peculiarities and gifts. In two massive novels, *Weymouth Sands* (1934) and *Maiden Castle* (1936), Powys treats of sexual sublimation directly and specifically, though with a characteristic lacing of humour. It may be coincidental that both he and Williams were eloquent lecturers, with the ability virtually to mesmerise their audiences; but both were conscious of their almost thaumaturgic powers and were wary of exploiting them. In his *Autobiography* (1934) Powys admits to sadistic fantasies (though he was never sadistic in practise), and *Letters to Lalage* raises the question as to how far there was a sadistic streak in Williams too. Certainly in Williams' novels, poems, and plays there is much stress on purgation through suffering; but this would in his case seem to spring from an acute awareness of the afflictions endemic to the lives of men and women on this planet, a torturing vision that Powys fully shared; though of the two of them it was Williams who was the more prepared to consider it worth enquiring why this should be so. (His essay "The Cross" is one of the very few theological statements that contrive to treat the question of evil and injustice without succumbing to the extremes either of shrill protest or of reverential complacency.)

Both Williams and Powys protected their sensitivity with an elaborate use of courtly manners and verbal qualifications; and in Williams' case the device coincided with his religious conviction as to the simultaneous value and imperfection of the human soul. But where his personal relationships were concerned, the bestowal of mythological names may at a purely human level have been a defence against intrusion. It is noteworthy that when Lois Lang-Sims declined the role of "Lalage," her own name was not thereby restored to her. Indeed, the omission of any preliminary address in his letters may be a further indication of shyness on Williams' part.

This shyness would have been dictated also by his awareness of how attractive he could be to women. As C. S. Lewis commented, "Women find him so attractive that if he were a bad man he could do what he liked either as a Don Juan or a charlatan." The character of Ransome in Lewis' *That Hideous Strength* (1945), a novel in which Williams' influence is much in evidence, gives a sense of the kind of impact he had upon such young women as the heroine Jane Studdock; and *Letters to Lalage* provides a real-life commentary on the fictitious situation. Not the least valuable aspect of this book is the way in which it provides an instance of an intelligent but troubled disciple endeavouring under a master's direction to put into practise two of his most distinctive doctrines, the Theology of Romantic Love and the Practise of Substituted Love. And when judged as specific practises it does not seem that either of them worked.

But to put the matter in this way is to employ a language of technology completely alien to the spiritual universe of which Williams was speaking. For him, romantic love and substituted love were spiritual laws in the way that gravity and thermodynamics were physical laws: they express the way things happen. People are, in painful fact and seeming injustice, always being substituted for each other; it is a law of necessity. All Williams asked of his friends was that they choose that necessity. The effective substitutions depicted in his novel *Descent into Hell* and his play *The House of the Octopus* are, of course, of his own devising; and it may be that the kind of substitution he asked of Lois Lang-Sims (and the one she more lightheartedly asked of him) were premature, tainted by too great a deliberation and self-awareness. The level of conscious exchange lies well below the surface of ordinary human relationships, and what may be true as a general principle is not to be automatically invoked upon a casual occasion. In this instance the real trouble may be that Williams did not know enough of his pupil as she really was. Their relationship was not based on an equality; and "Lalage" was more a figment of his own mind than she was Lois in the fullness of her being.

To raise this doubt is to raise it likewise in connection with the doctrine of Romantic Love. In her autobiography, Lois Lang-Sims sets down the difference between herself and Williams very plainly.

> There was an extraordinary similarity between our respective ways of looking at the world. The great difference between us—apart of course from Charles's vastly superior intellectual gifts—lay in his total neglect of a region of the mind which to me was of immense importance. His own soul was to him unknown. He simply assumed that his private myth and the images of which it was composed, including that of his "Beatrice," represented a divine communication from above rather than an objectivisation of that which lay hidden within himself.

The question that Lois Lang-Sims asked of Williams—*who* was to be the object of love?—while a necessary corrective to the extremes of idealism, may, however, seem to be beside the point that he was making. It is not *whom* but *how* one loves that matters (though, as her question indicates, the "how" necessarily dictates the "whom"). But Williams' doctrine allows for other than sexual adorations. His point would seem to be that the experience of falling in love is in fact a step justified by its very nature in so far as it affirms the essential (and thus potential) lovability of everything. For God creates the world because He loves it and in order that its human inhabitants should love each other. The experience of Romantic Love, as much as that of Substitution, expresses the nature of things; love, no less than pain, is of necessity, and it is a necessity that likewise has to be chosen. The experience of romantic love (or delight) is an apprehension of God's purpose for His world. It is less a process in time than a perspective on eternity; and as such (Williams knew this all too well) the vision is not to be confined to one person or one thing.

But the question of particularity remains. Williams displays remarkably little interest in the actual daily concerns of his correspondent: she is to be absorbed into his personal myth, but he is not prepared to participate in hers, any more than a regular confessor would do: he fulfills a priestly function. Not seeing him regularly, not forming part of his daily circle, she was compelled to play her role in isolation; and when she declined to play it further she was peremptorily, if courteously, dismissed. What was the reason for Williams' abrupt behaviour? My own guess would be—embarrassment. He had revealed his inmost need and fantasy to someone who refused to be held in the (almost literally) charmed circle; in his own words, "hemispheres altered place" and left him gasping for his native air. There is thus great pathos as well as puzzlement in the denoument. It is a singularly ironic instance of how a concern with the best can bring about the frustration of the good.

The encounter between Charles Williams and Lois Lang-Sims shows the interaction of two minds and temperaments who were alike enough to appreciate each other and different enough to sift each other's truth. The disciple's autobiography shows how drastically she could test herself, and how rigorously and painfully she searched for the truth that it was in her to find; in her own story the relationship with Williams was an important but not definitive stage. Where Williams himself was concerned, we have no knowledge of the impact that she made on him; but for his readers the correspondence (regrettably one-sided though it is, since her own letters have not survived) serves as an invaluable means of assessing not only the validity of two of Williams' most influential doctrines, but also the nature of the man he was. Lois Lang-Sims, while conscious of his strangeness, was yet more certain of his goodness. For others, the portrait that emerges is of a man who partook reassuringly of our all too maculate humanity, and of one who, no less than his admirers and disciples, and no less than the wife who chose thus to commemorate him, endured and realised the full implication of the words that mark his grave: Under the Mercy.

Glen Cavaliero

Letters to Lalage

THE LETTERS OF CHARLES WILLIAMS
TO LOIS LANG-SIMS
with a Commentary by
Lois Lang-Sims

The grave of Charles Williams in an Oxford churchyard is marked by a stone bearing his name and the terse description: *Poet,* followed by the words, *Under the Mercy.*

Charles himself wished to be remembered primarily as a poet, although it seems doubtful that this will be the case, or that his reputation could survive on such a foundation. He was, in fact, a metaphysician of genius who strove to communicate his personal vision by means of poetry, novels, his own peculiar brand of literary criticism (characterised always by a devotion to accuracy, clarity, and justice, but having a disconcerting tendency to depart from the immediate subject)—and, most importantly, two books which fall into no recognised category: *The Descent of the Dove* (a history of the workings of the Holy Spirit in the Church), and *The Figure of Beatrice.* The former is an exposition of the tremendous and little understood idea of the *Coinherence,* a word salvaged by Charles from the Early Fathers, at the same time as he distilled out of their writings the complex meaning it represents, the latter a profound study of romantic love in its relation to the metaphysical teachings underlying the orthodoxy of the Church.

Under the Mercy is a phrase that appears frequently in his writings, as it did in his conversation. He liked to refer to the Divinity by Its Attributes: the Mercy, the Protection, the Omnipotence. In his personal life he seemed always to be clinging to the faith that, balanced as he was upon the knife-edge of his Christian allegiance in the world of myth and magic that his passion-inflamed imagination had conjured up, he would find at last, in death if by no other route, the stillness of the Love of God. It was his wife, Michal, in one of those sudden flashes of crystal-clear insight of which she was not infrequently capable, who chose the inscription on the stone. Nothing could have been more appropriate.

Nowadays the name of Charles Williams tends to be associated with those of J. R. R. Tolkien and C. S. Lewis. The three men were friends, meeting regularly during the war years when Charles was living in Oxford. Lewis had an admiration for Charles amounting to hero-worship: this influence is apparent in his work; it has since emerged that Tolkien was antagonised by what he regarded as the undiscriminating devotion of one of his two friends for the other. Neither Lewis nor Tolkien were original thinkers: their popularity depends upon a fashion which rates academic fantasy-weaving above the capacity to move freely in the realm of ideas. Charles Williams will be remembered when they are forgotten. In the meantime, the association is misleading; and, in fact, when one looks around for his true companions, no name suggests itself. He stands very much on his own, his myth-making imagination tempered by a byzantine clarity of definition that discourages what is, in some respects, the most obvious comparison—with the George MacDonald of *Phantastes* and *Lilith*. In 1983 his reputation was well served by Glen Cavaliero's scholarly and balanced assessment, *Charles Williams: Poet of Theology*. Other publications have been less useful. But anyone who takes it upon him or herself to introduce others to a writer so passionately and personally involved in his own thought-world, even to the extent of manipulating his friends into fulfilling the roles created for them in his private myth, is faced with an initial problem. No matter what may be said to the effect that a writer's output should be assessed without reference to his personal character and the circumstances of his life, in the case of Charles Williams it is all but impossible to disentangle the one from the other, since the one continuously proceeded out of the other, in a way that can only with difficulty be understood by anyone who was never personally involved in his experiments.

For Charles did indeed carry out experiments in connection with his friends—with deep sincerity and for a high purpose always; but also, it must be said, with a certain methodical ruthlessness that was not altogether pleasant. These experiments were then transposed into his work. The work must be assessed, in the first place, as it stands of course. But it will be more fully and easily understood insofar as it can be related to the private mythology that was being constructed alongside it.

It is to this end that I have decided to present, complete and unabridged, a series of letters representing, in what is perhaps an exceptionally compressed and intensive form, one such experiment, carried out over a period of approximately six months. There could be no better illustration of the kind of odd, ambiguous demands that were made by Charles upon some, though not all, of the women with whom he entered into a master-disciple relationship. He made these demands because, from some cause hidden deep in his nature, he needed the creative power that he derived from their fulfillment. Without that power he could not work. Essentially, it was a power derived from the consciously directed holding in check of the passions associated with romantic love: this does not, however, mean that he was "in love" with all the women who became for him the vehicles of this mysterious force. Charles was only ever in love with two women: his wife and the lady he called "Phillida" or "Celia" (the latter name being the one to which he attached the more intimate significance, though neither were her own). Certain other women were chosen by him as "types" of his Lady, precisely as in the *Taliessin* poems, the slave girl is a type of Dindrane, the beloved of the King's poet (with whom Charles identified himself). He needed these substitutes when, for long periods and a variety of causes, neither his wife nor his "Celia" were available to play the role for which first the one and then the other had been cast.

All of which sounds very much more unscrupulous than in fact it was. I cannot absolve Charles altogether from the charge of unscrupulousness; but only those who knew him can realise the extent to which he was conscious of the necessity of holding an infinitely delicate balance which, if lost, would precipitate him into the realm of madness, that place of the mind which in his *Taliessin* poems he called P'o-lu. P'o-lu was, for him, the antithesis of Byzantium, the mythical and mystical Empire that represented the "organic body," the Coinherence. P'o-lu was the terrifying wilderness, the "upside-down" of the world, leading to the ultimate hell that awaited those who sought power for power's own sake.

> Inarticulate always on an inarticulate sea
> beyond P'o-lu the headless Emperor moves,
> the octopuses round him; lost are the Roman hands;
> lost are the substantial instruments of being. . . .

Charles never lost sight of that image. It represented the ever-present possible-impossibility within himself. Because of it, he never attempted to persuade anyone—lover, disciple, colleague, or friend—to follow him spiritually, intellectually, or physically one step further than he or she was genuinely willing to go. Those of us of whom much was demanded knew that we had only to hesitate for an instant and the demand would be withdrawn.

There was a price to be paid in that event; and, as will be seen, I learnt what it was; but that Charles desired anything of anyone that was not a gift freely given, no one who knew him even a little can ever have supposed. An odd kind of wry humor, entirely peculiar to himself, tempered every manifestation of what might, without it, have seemed like an exercise of power; and, with it, became something so delicately paradoxical that no single word can describe it.

It was not until after his death that I was introduced into his circle of friends. This happened as a result of his having left with one of them a list of people to be informed in the event of his being killed in a raid. My name was on this list. In this way I found the answers to a number of questions by which I had previously been perplexed. I discovered that I was not by any means the only person who had been cast as a "stand-in" for Phillida in her absence. (Phillida had married and gone away; moreover the violence of Charles's passion for her may well have precluded the possibility of a sustained relationship such as those he pursued with her substitutes. The essence of the experiment was restraint. Confronted by a woman with whom he was not physically in love, this would have cost him no more in terms of emotional disturbance than he was prepared to expend. He was, after all, in search of creative power to be used in his work. Phillida had come near to destroying him: her flight from the situation was probably motivated as much by concern for him as for herself.) At the same time I realised that my own experience could have been unique, in that I was apparently the only one who had had no dealings with Charles in any more everyday context. The others had all of them, it seemed, been his personal friends—colleagues at the Oxford University Press, students of his classes on English literature, or simply people who had gravitated towards him on account of an affinity of interests. All of them had met and corresponded with him in a variety of situations, socially, personally, in connection with their work. They had known each other. What some of them did not know, until I produced a furor by daring to mention it, was that aspect of "C. W." (as they tended to call him) that was all I had ever been permitted to experience.

Tentatively, I tried to discover if Charles had at any time been involved with the practices of ritual magic within a fellowship established for that purpose, since even my own slender knowledge of the subject suggested that this must have been the case. Charles was no dabbler in the occult. He understood its dangers; and confronted them with that Christian orthodoxy that secretes within itself all mysteries and all knowledge, and the antidotes to the darker mysteries and the more fearful sorts of knowledge. But still it was apparent that he had somewhere been instructed in matters that would not have been purveyed to him through any channels normally open within the church. It was in this context, I felt, that one should look for the key to his experiments. However, it became clear that, whether or not my guess was correct, his friends knew nothing about it, and were not particularly pleased with the suggestion. It was not until some years later that his onetime membership of the Order of the Golden Dawn was somehow brought to light; when this happened, there was a general tendency to underplay the importance of this episode in his life, almost as if it had been a sort of youthful prank. Charles joined the Order in 1917, and was an active member until 1928.[1] The Golden Dawn was, in its time, in this country, the most well-known and genuinely knowledgeable confraternity of its kind to be available to serious students. Charles had an amazing capacity for assimilating, synthesising, and remembering information. He must have learnt a great deal in those eleven years; and what he took from external sources would have touched hidden springs within himself. His reasons for leaving the Order are not known. Perhaps he sensed dangers; perhaps he was simply unwilling to admit another human being into the secrets of his inner life. I am certain as one can be of anything, that no one ever really penetrated beneath the mask-like image that Charles presented of himself—not Michal, not Phillida, certainly not his would-be Masters in the brotherhood of the Golden Dawn, who were at least as unlikely to have gained any personal influence over him as the vicar of his parish church.

I met Michal eventually through his friends, though it could not be said that a great deal of love was lost between her and the group of people whom she regarded as having connived at his love affair with someone else. Charles had never been physically unfaithful to Michal; but that, understandably, was a minor matter in her eyes compared with the final transference of the romantic adoration bestowed upon her during their long courtship and the early years of their married life. Total rage against Phillida burned in her most, but not all, of the time. When it was not burning it was nonexistent. One never knew with Michal, from one moment to the next, which Michal she was deciding to be. I used to say that, with one exception, Charles was the strangest human being I had ever met in my life: the one exception was Michal. Michal, in different moods, could display

---

[1]R. A. Gilbert in *The Golden Dawn* (Aquarian Press, 1983) reveals that what Charles actually joined was an offshoot of the original Order entitled the Fellowship of the Rosy Cross inaugurated in 1915 by A. E. Waite.

the passions of a maenad and the cool detachment of a sphinx. Like Charles (and this seemed to be the one characteristic they had in common, besides being one they shared with no one else), her personality was interiorised to such an extent that nothing in her outward environment reflected it by so much as a hint. The Hampstead flat where the two of them had lived for the greater part of their married life, struck me, when I visited it, as being a sort of mental desert, containing nothing that one could think of as having been valued or even noticed by its occupants. One expects to be told something when one enters someone else's home. If the message is merely that its owner is conventional, conformist, wishing to be slotted inconspicuously into a particular social category, at least that is a message of a sort. One recognises the category if nothing else. In Michal's flat I felt that I was being told nothing. The furniture was noncommittal. The few prints on the walls were noncommittal. There were hardly any books: Michal, I thought, must have got rid of Charles's library, perhaps because it reminded her of those areas of his life from which she felt left out. Michal's clothes, too, were noncommittal, as had been Charles's pinstripe suits, rolled umbrella, and city businessman's homburg hat. She herself was a striking-looking woman, tall, well-built, with dark hair and eyes, one of those people who, without appearing at first sight to be in the least fascinating, prove to have the power to fascinate. I found her physically disturbing, in a way that I tried to describe by saying that I felt as if her body and her psyche had somehow got out of alignment: occasionally, and no doubt absurdly, I would have the notion that she was not precisely where she appeared to be but somewhere else in the room. For the first six months or so of our acquaintance, I adored Michal; but adoring Michal was not an enviable experience. One could be her dearest friend one day, and twenty-four hours later find oneself being scathed by her contempt, the object of her unmitigated disgust. Charles once said in praise of his wife that she was a woman who never passed judgements: the remark was, as might have been expected, strictly accurate. Michal did not judge; she merely, when she felt inclined to do so, spat.

The circle, as it was sometimes called, of Charles's friends was composed of the original "Companions of the Coinherence," who were also described by Charles as the "household" within the context of the Taliessin myth. Being counted as one of the household did not necessarily, however, involve being privy to all its secrets. As a result of my indiscretions (if such they were) those who had never been involved in Charles's more unusual practices must have suffered a severe shock. Inevitably there were misunderstandings and disagreements. Some people felt strongly that the matter need never be publicly exposed. I was almost unanimously condemned for the incomplete and restrained account of my relationship with Charles which appears in my autobiography, *A Time to be Born*. (That account contains one or two inexcusable inaccuracies: I state, for instance, that Charles wrote to me "almost every day," which was never the case.) Since then, students of Charles's work have inevitably begun to probe into and speculate upon the more problematical aspects of his personal life. My own view is that they should be assisted in the task by those who know what they are talking about. How else can one hope, in the end, for a just assessment of the man as he really was?

I first heard of Charles Williams by the name, not commonly in use among his disciples, of "Chas. Bill."

In the early 1930s my cousin Margery and I, being rivals in all things, were in the habit of exchanging accounts of what went on at our respective schools. In this contest I was basically in the stronger position. Because I genuinely believed that mine was the best of all schools, I did not really mind admitting that Margery's was an altogether more prestigious establishment. Downe House was, in fact, the one fashionable and expensive girls' school, in the thirties, to offer its pupils a really valuable education in literature, drama, and the arts, together with the inculcation of an almost morbidly self-conscious morality and high-mindedness. Its founder, Miss Olive Willis, was a woman of strong character and high intelligence. Among those of her personal friends whose services she enlisted on behalf of her school were Dame Myra Hess, whose regular piano recitals must have been a great boost to its reputation—and Charles Williams.

Charles wrote a play (*A Myth of Bacon*) for the girls of Downe House to perform in their Greek theatre (in those days a rarefied and original amenity at the thought of which I was suitably impressed). It was, however, in his capacity as a lecturer on English poetic drama that Chas. Bill, as they called him, was most fervently appreciated by the pupils of Miss Willis. No professional clown, it would seem, could have beaten his performances. In graphic imitation of his antics, my cousin would stride up and down an imaginary stage, grimacing like a maniacal monkey, clasping her arms about her as she mimicked his habit of seizing one of the stage curtains in a wild embrace while the school held its breath. "We always think it's going to come down on his head when he does that, but it hasn't—yet." Then, when I laughed, she would add firmly, in case I should underestimate the significance of having their own celebrity to be laughed at:

"Of course, he's a famous poet. And I told you, didn't I, about him and Miss Willis?"

"I don't remember exactly." (This was untrue; but I knew what was expected of me, and besides I liked the little story.) "Tell me again."

"Well, someone was looking out of the window, and Chas. Bill and Miss Willis were in the garden. And he gave her a rose and she gave him a kiss."

Trying to visualise my own head mistress exchanging roses and kisses with visiting lecturers or indeed with anyone whatsoever at any time, I conceded yet another point in favour of Downe House. Nothing could be more typical of Charles than the picture this story conjures up. I have since wondered if Miss Willis, in common with a number of other women who were thé recipients of such romantic flourishes as this, understandably imagined herself to be more important to him than she really was.

I left school, and for some years forgot about "Chas. Bill." When I remembered him again it was in a context so completely new that I even visualised him quite differently, no longer as a personification of the lunatic, the lover, and the poet, clasping curtains, presenting roses, but as an ascetic, gentle old man with a snow-white pointed beard, dispensing wisdom. It was wartime; and I had joined the congregation of St. George's church in Canterbury, where a small group of us were dedicated to the pursuit of Christian socialism combined with folk dancing, madrigals, and a general rethinking of the tenets of the Establishment. T. S. Eliot, Charles Williams, and C. S. Lewis were a much admired trio, tending to be grouped together in our minds; although in the case of Eliot much had to be, and was, overlooked for the sake of his Canterbury play in which some of us had taken part. *Murder in the Cathedral* had been followed, a year later, by Charles Williams' *Thomas Cranmer of Canterbury,* likewise commissioned for the Friends' Festival and performed in the Chapter House. However, by the time of my arrival on the scene, the war having started, such theatrical excitements had been relegated to the past. I had never caught a glimpse of Charles Williams. Had I done so even once in the distance, no snow-white-bearded gentleman could have found his way into my thoughts.

In those days I read with avidity the novels, *Cranmer, The Descent of the Dove,* and, of course, the *Taliessin* poems, these last understood very dimly in the way that one glimpses something out of the corner of an eye. More deeply than by any of these I was impressed by a short passion play for radio entitled *The Three Temptations,* broadcast on Good Friday at a time when I was feeling more than usually downcast, terrified by the bombs and riven by a love affair that had gone wrong. One line from this play repeated itself over and over in my mind:

I must unknow Thee that these others may know Thee.

That, I thought, was great poetry and a great prayer. I still think so.

In 1943 *The Figure of Beatrice* was published. I was twenty-six. I remember buying the book at Zwemmer's in Charing Cross Road, opening it as I went through the door, and starting to read it in the street. Its theme was of absorbing interest to me at that time: I was cherishing an unrequited love which made me excessively miserable, although it must be said that I preferred to be miserable rather than to get over it, which I could have done at any moment.

The Figure of Beatrice is surely Charles's greatest book. In it he digs deep into the metaphysical meaning of romantic love. Having read it carefully more than once, I wrote to him with a question, which must now be reconstructed from memory since I no longer have my side of our correspondence. The fundamental idea of the book is that of the lover's perception of the beloved as he or she exists eternally in the Mind of God. So Dante, being caught up into the state of love, was enabled to see in the face and form of his Beatrice an apparition of ideal beauty which would lead him eventually to the verge of the beatific vision itself—provided he remained faithful to the truth of what he had seen, permitting neither his own passions nor the flaws in the character of the human Beatrice, as these must inevitably be experienced, to deflect him from his chosen path. That path was defined by Charles as the Way of Affirmation of Images, as distinct from the *Via Negativa* of imageless contemplation typified by a John of the Cross. My problem, when I sat down to write my first letter to Charles, was the same as when, six months later, I faced him across the stewed greengages in the dining room of the Randolph Hotel, and told him that he was leaving the *person* of the beloved out of account. *Who,* I demanded on both occasions to know, was supposed to be the *object* of love in the Dantean experience?

According to Charles, as I understood it, the human Beatrice of the here and now, recognised and fully accepted as she must be, with all her faults, was not *in herself* the object of her lover's adoration, which was fixed upon Beatrice "in her glory," the ideal Beatrice of the heavenly state. But, I pointed out, one could not be absolutely certain that Beatrice was, ever had been, or ever would be, in that state. I reminded Charles of a character in his own novel, *Descent into Hell*. If Wentworth could be consigned to hell, what became of his "glory?" Had it ever even existed? Wentworth was, of course, a fictional character; but he represented the Church's teaching that the *possibility* of damnation, however remote and unthinkable, is a necessary corollary of free will. I was driving logic to its limits, but—I did not want to be in love with an hypothesis. I wanted the object of my love to be the person-as-he-was-in-himself. Painstakingly, I built up a picture of an imaginary character whom I called Jane. Jane was the object of love. But her lover could not be absolutely sure that Jane would not finally choose as Wentworth had chosen, in which case (according to Charles) he would have been loving someone—or something—that had never been in existence; and then again, Wentworth himself must have been lovable once: if Wentworth, as a child, had been loved, Charles must admit that it could not have been his "glory" that was the object of that love.

A very laborious letter it must have been; although somehow I fancy that I expressed my perplexity more simply and spontaneously then than now—perhaps because I was genuinely perplexed, whereas now I see the matter in a rather different light.

———————————

Oxford University Press
Southfield House
Oxford
9 Sept./43

Dear Miss Lang-Sims,

I was certain that I should have to try and answer your question sooner or later, so don't apologise. It's a most proper question; and now what do I say?

Well, first we might rule out Hell. If Jane ever reached that (by definition) final state, I can't say what might happen to her 'glory'. Or only as a speculation. All we have to deal with is the present situation.

(2) I am not very keen on dividing Jane's soul from her body, or indeed eternity from time. Jane is a whole organism, and (as far as possible) I love the whole organism which is Jane. Probably, in fact, I shall find I am largely attracted by Jane's physical and mental sides and have a very faint idea of her spiritual. However . . . But it is certain that without a body there is no Jane; except indeed between death and the Resurrection.

(3) What I see, then, is Jane-in-her-glory—or as much as I can take in: Jane as God devised her, or at least to some extent Jane as God devised

Charles Williams writing a letter in the garden at Oxford. Photograph, John Spalding

her. On the other hand, when Jane snaps her sister's head off, or indulges in malicious gossip, or whatever, it is clear that Jane is not being as God devised her. I do not find myself able to deny either fact. (The same thing has been noticed by those people who have done either you or me the honour of admiring us.)

It is up to Jane to become as glorious (by her own will assisting) in all her moments as God devised her to be by his. This, we all agree, is a long business; and her adorers may not be much help, for they are often apt to mix up their own personal tastes with truth of judgement. Presumably God knows what he meant Jane to be like, and allows us to see a hint of that.

(4) The will is asserted to be a spiritual capacity. But it is, of course, since Jane is a human being and therefore fallen—but still retaining (as the doctors teach us) something of her originally-intended powers—precisely the spiritual capacities which are fallen. They are capacities like the phys-

ical (which are also clouded) of the one organic Jane. I am sure we must not divide her. I am also sure that until Jane *is* damned—God forbid!—we can go on believing that we saw Jane-in-her-glory. However maddening Jane is. I should add, merely as a precaution, that we had better be very careful about this. The maddeningness of Jane is generally due to our fallen nature as much as to hers. Or more. And I should hate any doctrine which deflected an ardent attention to Jane, the single organic Jane.

I'm not sure that this is any use, but it will show good-will. I do not write as final doctrine but as merely suggestion towards our exploring of these high mysteries . . . (I think Jane must be a delightful creature now we have composed her so carefully.) Pray contradict me anywhere, if you wish.

Very sincerely yours,
Charles Williams

I wrote again pursuing the discussion.

Southfield House
Oxford
20 Sept. 1943

Dear Miss Lang-Sims,

If you send me a postcard with a quotation from Shaw's *Caesar and Cleopatra*—Caesar's remark: 'Do you presume to encourage me?'—I shall understand. For indeed I do not know that I am doing anything else—shyly, though with some persistence.

It seems to me—I take my courage in both hands—that your dispositions are admirable; and I very much hope you will never go back on them, spiritually or intellectually. I mean particularly this business of Jane mattering infinitely and yet not mattering at all; of practising a virtue with the intention of another profiting; of one relationship being pursued in others. One must continually build an altar, and then (nine to one) the fire from heaven will come down somewhere else. I have written somewhere that *that* was what was wrong with Cain; he too much expected the fire on his own. The Kingdom demands not only virtues but a courtesy in virtue, a lightness of touch, style. Humility? I suppose it is simply humility, but the poor word is so heavy nowadays. Your letters have had more than a touch of this; continue, I beg you, to practise it so.

You know St. Thomas, quoting Boethius, defined eternity as 'the perfect *and simultaneous* possession of everlasting life'? I was rather struck (besides the compliment!) by your allusion to Wentworth; of course you are quite right. But, since all time is present to eternity (or in, or whatever we ought to say) I suppose the adorable baby Wentworth, as the adorable present Jane or Beatrice, is in eternity; it is in the Kingdom at this moment. What future moments may be . . . if Jane or Wentworth insists on encouraging that of which God says 'I never knew you' . . . but that is a future moment and not more real than this. No second experience can destroy the validity of a first experience, if (as we believe) it was truly valid.

Of course I agree about loving for the sake of God—that is, because God loves; though the realization of this duty as distinguished from the intellectual knowledge of it is apt to be a chilly moment. Still, there it is . . though even Jane is apt to be a little remote about it. I cannot think why I should dislike to be loved on principle . . at least, I can; the Fall and all that.

This adds nothing, but it does mean to be a prayer to you to continue in the Way. Some years ago there was begun a Company . . scattered and unknown to each other . . called of the Co-inherence, and when I can find a copy of the Promulgation I will, if you choose, send it. It involves you in nothing more than you are already involved in; that is its great charm. These things are all—I mean, what we have been writing about—more important than our personal convenience; not that your letters are the least inconvenience—they aren't. I do not know if you are ever likely to be in Oxford, or could come; if so, we might lunch and discuss. I am tied here for the period of the war, though I frequently rush up to my people for week-ends. But we could probably fix one of these if it were more convenient. This, however, only in case you should be able or wish to do so.

All blessings
C. W.

The Headquarters of the Oxford University Press had been moved to Oxford for the duration of the war. Charles had worked for the Press for thirty-five years; it had been the scene of his friendship with Phillida. In his mythical world it was sometimes Byzantium, sometimes Camelot (the one being an extension of the other in the Taliessin poems, "each in each," according to the principle expressed in the great idea of the Coinherence), with Sir Humphrey Milford in the alternating roles of the Emperor and the High King. Michal having refused to leave London, Charles had gone to live with the Spalding family in South Parks Road. When he entertained guests, he generally borrowed the table at the Randolph Hotel which was permanently reserved for two of his friends who were staying there as residents.

Of course I accepted his invitation. My mother and I had left Canterbury and gone to live in a tumbledown old cottage near Thaxted in Essex. My mother was in the early stages of Parkinson's disease: the state of her health was a constant source of anxiety and bewilderment to me, no diagnosis of her illness having so far been produced.

Southfield House
Oxford
5 Oct. /43

My dear Miss Lang-Sims,

I have been away from Oxford during the week-end, which shall excuse the delay in answering.

What about the week after next? I am going to lecture on Tuesdays in the mornings, and I go to London on that Friday afternoon. But I imagine the journey from Thaxted must be so horrid and long that you wouldn't be likely to get here much before lunch, so that would leave Tuesday also free, if you chose. (Or, of course, if you were here before 11, come to the lecture—but you won't be.) Anyhow, pick your day between Monday 15 October and Thursday 18 October inclusive. And let me know.

This place is so far from the city's centre that we must try and arrange to meet, though unknown, nearer. But that we can, no doubt, manage.

Thank you for St. George; I hadn't seen it. And I liked the poem. Substitute 'magnificence and modesty' in my vocabulary for 'splendour and homeliness' in yours, and behold agreement! (Though I do like living in cities if you will excuse me.)

I send you the . . I don't quite know what to call it . . the Promulgation of the Company. No one knows anyone, or only by holy luck, so you will see how unorganised it is. But we can talk. There is a poem on the same idea in some new *Taliessins,* but I haven't seen proofs yet.

As for youth—the hierarchies change always, and debt is always mutual.

Yours,
C. W.

Charles's acknowledgment of "St. George" refers to a booklet commemorating the church of St. George the Martyr in Canterbury, which had been destroyed by fire in 1942. The rector's wife, hearing of my correspondence with Charles, had asked me to send him a copy; and to please her I had done so. The fact that, even then, before our first meeting, I experienced an odd feeling of unwillingness, as if I were doing something inappropriate, shows how I sensed from the very start the nature of his intentions towards me. The contents of the little booklet, including my own poem, were such as might have been expected to arouse his sympathy and interest: his own name was mentioned with gratitude. But in sending him something extraneous to our correspondence, suggesting involvements which had nothing to do with my commitment to him, I was stepping outside the role that was already being created for me in his myth. Quite unanalysable at the time had been that faint, all but unadmitted hesitancy: now, as I try to analyse it, I realise both how nonsensical in rational terms it was, and how it was to be confirmed again and again in the ensuing months.

"Splendour with homeliness" was a phrase used by one contributor (not, incidentally, myself) to describe the ideal manner of conducting sacred rites. Charles's remark about "cities" refers to my poem, which contained a rather banal comment on "the squalor of living in cities. . . . Cities full of hate. . . ." Canterbury was certainly full of hate (as also of love); but in fact I adored it and was never really happy anywhere else. However, I was no poet.

The Promulgation of the Company was as follows:

1. The order has no constitution except in its members. As it was said: Others he saved, himself he cannot save.

2. It recommends nevertheless that its members shall make a formal act of union with it and of recognition of their own nature. As it was said: Am I my brother's keeper?

3. Its concern is the practice of the apprehension of the Co-inherence both as a natural and a supernatural principle. As it was said: Let us make man in Our image.

4. It is therefore *per necessitatem,* Christian. As it was said: And whoever says there was when this was not, let him be anathema.

5. It recommends therefore the study, on the contemplative side, of the Co-inherence of the Holy and Blessed Trinity, of the Two Natures in the Single Person, of the Mother and Son, of the communicated Eucharist, and of the whole Catholic Church. As it was said: *figlia del tuo figlio.* And on the active side, of methods of exchange, in the State, in all forms of love, and in all natural things, such as childbirth. As it was said: Bear ye one another's burdens.

6. It concludes in the Divine Substitution of Messias all forms of exchange and substitution, and it invokes this Act as the root of all. As it was said: He must become, as it were, a double man.

7. The Order will associate itself primarily with four feasts: the Feast of the Annunciation, the Feast of the Blessed Trinity, the Feast of the Transfiguration, and the Commemoration of All Souls. As it was said: Another will be in me and I in him.

Southfield House
11 Oct. /43

Dear Miss Lang-Sims,

That will be admirable. I will do something about lunch, but it does occur to me that if we could see each other first we should know whom to look for. I am staying in Oxford at 9 South Parks Rd.—which you may

know. Anyhow, if you could give yourself the trouble of calling there—
perhaps about ten?—on the Thursday morning, we could exchange a word
before I come here. Thus making life a little less complex. And if I remember to have it with me, I will lend you the new Taliessin poem on the
Founding of the Company.

Till when, and blessings,
always yours,
C. W.

As I rang the bell of the house in South Parks Road I
could hear a clock striking inside: it was ten o'clock; exactly to the minute the time of my appointment. The clock
was still striking as the door was flung open, and my private fantasy of Charles was annihilated on the instant, as
I found myself being whirled into the house. Almost before I knew what was happening, I was in the drawing
room, gazing up at Charles in the utmost astonishment.
He was standing over me in an attitude that was somehow
at the same time deferential and authoritarian, in that sin-
gular equilibrium of opposites that I would come to know
as being uniquely his. Charles, in his middle fifties, was a
grey-haired, fragile-looking man, with a deeply creased,
abnormally sensitive face which seemed to exist only in
movement. He talked out of the side of his mouth, a habit
which resulted in a peculiar grimace and seemed to em-
phasize his odd accent and the unattractive resonance of
his voice. I was held by his gaze, which had a quality of
intent stillness wholly at variance with the rapid flow of
words and the constant jerky movement of his limbs and
the muscles of his face. For the first few moments I was
so stunned by the total impact of the man that I took in
neither the details of his appearance nor the meaning of
what he had said. I only began to recover myself when,
withdrawing his gaze from my riveted eyes, he flung himself sideways into a chair, his legs over the arm, and his
head screwed round in a posture so odd that in anyone
else—let alone any other middle-aged gentleman in a pin-
striped suit—it would have made me want to laugh.

Charles, however, could behave ludicrously without ever being ludicrous: even the pupils of Downe House, astounded by the antics of "Chas. Bill," had never seen him as being that. For his was a dignity that outsoared absurdity; as his was an attractiveness so potent that it turned the ugliness of his voice and features to no account. (In the same way, I have found myself thinking that in him there burned a flame of pure sanctity that redeemed not only his eccentricities but even the seeming ruthlessness of his methods and his experiments.)

I perceived that I was, for some reason, greatly approved. There was nothing I needed to say or to do, except to sit still and give my entire attention, not so much to the meaning of his speech, which was too fast, and its content too compressed, for me to have followed it at all easily even had I been in a less bemused state, but simply to the fact that I was being addressed. As I could not in any case have said a word, and as I was transfixed where I sat and would hardly have noticed if an angel had materialised in front of us, my situation was in no way difficult.

It was not until I had been courteously dismissed, and found myself walking slowly towards the city centre, to occupy my time as best I could until one o'clock, that I began to think. When I did, I was astonished at myself. I felt that I had committed myself to Charles, without in the least understanding what that commitment was going to involve. Something had happened between us; and now I must discover the nature of what had happened, and contrive to endure it since it could not be undone. For Charles himself, I found that I was experiencing a mixture of feelings. Love and veneration had been aroused in me without my knowing how or why; for these reactions had nothing to do with his books (I had almost forgotten the existence of his books). At the same time I was aware of being enspelled; and this was uncomfortable: I did not care to be enspelled. Over and beneath it all, more poignantly real to me than any other emotion at that moment, was something that I had never expected to feel and could hardly believe in when I realised what it was—a sharp-stinging ache of compassion for a being who had violently impressed me as being, humanly speaking, *alone*. For I knew even then that Charles was incapable of what I at least understood as being a human relationship on a personal basis. I sensed that he was totally identified with, and enclosed within, his own myth. The fragile, inadequate body that so clearly was in the process of being destroyed by a spirit too strong and fiery to be contained within the limitations of the flesh, had about it a quality of untouchability which recalled to me a passage in his verse:

'It is a doubt if my body is flesh or fish,'
he sang in his grief; 'hapless the woman who loves me,
hapless I . . .'

In the lounge of the Randolph Hotel, having lunched, Charles and I sat together on a sofa while he took my wrist and counted on my fingers the command: "Love—obey—pray—play—and be intelligent."

The hand which held mine quivered as if from a succession of electric shocks: it seemed to me that this quivering must be running through his entire body, finding an outlet in his hands. At lunch we—he, mostly—had talked of Beatrice in the City, of the City as an extended image of Beatrice, of Canterbury and the man with whom I was in love as types of both or rather of that reality for which both stood. Now he was seeming to assume, in deadly earnest and yet as a kind of game, that I would obey his commands because I was bonded to him within the Company to which I belonged by virtue of what he called my "task." (It was indeed true that for three years before I read Charles's exposition of romantic love I had consciously tried to practise exactly the kind of interior exercises it prescribes, whether as a genuine spiritual discipline or, partially at least, as a form of self-indulgence, it is up to anyone to question: Charles himself did not ask that sort of question.) My mind was in a swirl of unverbalised ideas that seemed as if they were gyrating in and out of some dimension beyond that in which I was physically present. The surprised and interested glances of

Lois Lang-Sims. Photograph taken shortly before her first meeting with Charles Williams.

the other occupants of the lounge no longer impinged upon me (as they had done when I first arrived and we sat over drinks before lunch; and as they would do, fleet-ingly, again; though never again to produce any real dis-quiet—for what would have been the use?).

We collected and donned our outdoor things, and nego-tiated the swing doors on our way out. I shall never forget those doors, which featured in every one of my subse-quent meetings with Charles, because of the peculiar way he went through them, as if they were the curtains of the royal chamber to be swept ceremoniously aside for our exit or entrance. We parted on the steps of the hotel. Taking my hand, he fixed upon me a look which drove a wounding pain into my heart. Pain, I felt, was going to be an inescapable part of my association with this man. Then, with a combination of ritual solemnity, old-fashioned courtesy, and whimsical playfulness that no one but he could have produced, he bent over my hand and kissed it—and was gone, as swiftly and disconcertingly as if he had been a ghost. (I remember, on a later occasion, repeating to myself the line: "He had softly and suddenly vanished away, for the Snark *was* a Boojum, you see," and thinking crazily—one felt a bit crazy after sessions with Charles—that perhaps he did look for Snarks and see Boojums in that strange dimension he seemed partially to inhabit, along with Lewis Carroll himself.)

On the journey back to London the rhythm of the train beat out in my mind like a spell (and maybe, I thought, it *was* a kind of spell) those words:

"Love—obey—pray—play—and be intelligent."

Southfield House
27 Oct/43

My dear Lois,

How admirable of you!—and how merely proper! But now I am in something of a dilemma. I don't, on the one hand, wish to intrude; I don't, on the other, wish you to be working by yourself—since indeed you are so working at such serious tasks. It was never (at least in the myth) the habit of Taliessin to leave unrecognized the efforts of his peers.

So you can neglect this as much as you choose, and I certainly will not be churlish. On the other hand, I have the general feeling that we have only begun the discussion—to say nothing of the obedience. As you can, you must come to Oxford again. I want to know the history of your own discoveries. I want you to know that (if you choose) you are at work, within the Church, for the Company, and for (kissing your hand on it) Us. A superfluity, of course; but how much a needful superfluity!

Surveying then your engagements—and unless you contradict or are silent, We regard you as engaged to Us—there are these:

1) You are engaged to have in your mind the twin images of your friend, like Pauline and her twin in the *Descent*.[2] I am sure this is the best method, and to hold them so before God; not even begging too much that the one shall become the other, but this pause only that you may be of a quieter and stronger heart in the prayer of presentation—so to call it. Let the difficulty (so to speak) of their disagreement be turned inward to God as an operation without fuss. (Not that you do fuss.)

2) You are engaged to continue the work of substitution—and not to be surprised if you find yourself in some unexpected jam, interior or exterior; and to believe that it is of serious concern—to your friend, to yourself, to others (including Us, the least of your servants)—that you should.

3) You are engaged—and here particularly to me—to practise goodwill towards the mother, however wryly you smile while you do it, and however you seem to yourself to mess it up. I would far rather you seemed to mess it up than that you become a little over-conscious of your charity. No—I know, I know; but people do, and you or I may. But I know well—O very well indeed, Lois!—the distance and difficulty.

4) You are engaged to improve—by the charming way you said there was room for improvement; well, but it was charming!—your relations with your own mother. Lightly—ever, ever lightly! but no less certainly. And any other little tricks of sloth Your Excellency does us the honour of observing.

5) You are engaged to report—as a mythical slave or schoolgirl should—yes?—on your four jobs; or rather on (3) and (4)—the others will gain from it enough. Lightly, lightly, ever lightly! but no less certainly. Style, always style. If you are lazy or inattentive or negligent or a truant, why, you will say so as frankly as—may I say?—easily. Though I warn you I will have you, as frankly, pay for it.

There are five headings for the fingers of your other hand! But if you do not wish this sort of thing, tell me or do not even tell me. But if it seems to you for a year worth—making this movement? daring this discipline? practising this ritual? playing this game? then we all march at your service, and do you write out the five headings We gave you, and find yourself five words for the headings above, and send them. You are young and you are

---

[2]His novel, *Descent into Hell*.

wise at once; each in the other—Blanchfleur (who was Percivale's sister and foster-warden of Galahad) and a girl slave, so to name them in the Myth.

Blessings and thanks. In God,

C. W.

This is the first of his letters to me in which Charles uses the "royal We" in referring to himself. He did this always very carefully, to indicate when he was speaking in the capacity of what he sometimes called his "absurd lieutenancy" in the Company. It was a strange habit; but, in him, there was nothing quirky about it: it was the logical outcome of the whole system he had so methodically set up.

The "mother" referred to under his third heading, was of the man with whom I was in love. It seems that I had already told Charles a good deal of this particular story (I no longer remember exactly what I did tell him nor when: inevitably, since I no longer have my own letters, there are details in his that will have to be left unexplained). Unlike St. George's, this theme was not only acceptable but greatly encouraged, since it had been, and was to remain, the basis of my "task." It was on account of this that I had written to him in the first place.

So it was that I found myself committed to an obedience, the nature of which I did not really understand, within the context of a new kind of Religious Order, the mysterious Company into which I supposed myself to have been initiated, although I was unsure how or when (perhaps, I thought, it had been at that moment when, on the sofa at the Randolph, Charles had taken my hand and, turning it over, made the motion of writing something on the palm). Charles had presented me with the typescript of those of his new poems (later to be published as *The Region of the Summer Stars*) that were relevant to my own situation. These were *The Founding of the Company,* and the poems describing the relationship between the King's poet and the slave girl whom he sees as an image of the

Princess Dindrane whom he loves. (Dindrane was, of course, Phillida or Celia: in the poetry Taliessin loses her to a Convent, more acceptably than by her two successive marriages in real life.) I was, not surprisingly, confused and bemused by the way in which the "Company" appeared to be at the same time the "household" of the King's poet in Charles's own highly original version of the Arthurian myth, and the circle of his own personal friends. Dimly I perceived that the key to unraveling this confusion was to be found in Charles's total identification of the King's poet, Taliessin, with himself. Re-reading the poems today, my immediate reaction is to feel that never was there a more outrageous ego-trip in verse, nor a clearer example of the games people play for their own consolation and encouragement. And then, because I know this judgement is but half of the truth, and the other half is the more important—the other half is what made it possible for Charles to win the allegiance of his "household" not only in fantasy but in fact—I am ashamed. For who should know better than I do, that Charles was a man who immolated mind and body in the cause of achieving an infinitely delicate and accurate balance of the opposites, not in theory, not in the abstract, but in *himself?* In this fearful tension he chose, continuously, to live—and by it he was so severely torn that it was, I believe, the cause of his untimely death. That is what made him—as he was—a great human being and something akin to a saint.

Southfield House
Oxford
9 Nov./43

I was just considering writing to you—having lectured on *Hamlet* and lunched with a gentleman who does me the honour to admire *Beatrice,* and done a little Press work, and written to my wife—well, I was sitting back and saying to myself: 'Lois?' when a myrmidon appeared with your letter. Most admirable and suitable, and (as it were) generally agreeable all around.

Of course I allow the distinction. At least, I allow that till one has got out of the habit of sitting in the hole, one will not easily get into the habit of avoiding the hole. But I do not choose that you shall even trip into one (no, not though you do it five hundred times a day!), and as for sitting in one—O come, Nobility! and your excellency will copy out for me half a dozen times the 116th sonnet of the late Mr. Shakespeare, about the marriage of true minds, which does *not* mean two people, but the marriage of a mind to the universe, as I have said somewhere in *Beatrice*. And at the end you will add half a dozen times: 'and I shall have my ears soundly boxed for disobedience' (which you shall, next time you come). And send it all to me.

Let me know when you are free, and we will fix a day. And thank you for the prayer: it is a lovely thing. Your Excellency will remember the City always—and you might add to your mediations the phrase: 'Christ, the City, incorporate me.' And be (as far as may be) gay and happy.

I am your servant always. Be Ours; build Camelot in Thaxted. Thank you for everything. Be blessed.

C. W.

It will be noted that Charles begins this letter straight off, without an opening formula of address. Whether or not this was a general habit of his, I took it at the time as being both a great convenience and a mild rebuke. Finding it no longer possible to address him as "Mr. Williams," I had hesitantly written "Dear Charles," feeling that this was somehow an inappropriate mode of address within the context of the strange relationship he had imposed upon us, but that there was really nothing else to do. Charles seemed to say that there was something else to do: that is to say—nothing. From then onwards I never addressed him by any name, either in writing or face to face.

That winter I wrote to him every day; and every day, wet or fine, I bicycled into Thaxted to see if there was a letter waiting for me at the post office. Oddly, for his handwriting resembled the peregrinations of some small, methodical insect, I never found his letters hard to read; although if one did become baffled by a word, prolonged inspection of it was of no use: one read Charles's letters by the method of simply going straight into them by an act of faith.

Southfield House
12 Nov./43

Yes, I did get your first letter and meant to acknowledge and ratify it in mine. And then (but partly through thinking of you) forgot. Of course I approve. You shall give yourself the further trouble to think out from the prayers five single words to correspond to our other five; no hurry. And your left palm shall be for a Reformatory and your right for Camelot. And whenever, most admired Lady, you fall into a hole (even inadvertently), you will make the smallest dot in pencil on each palm. But with half a smile, however rueful. And if they seem to mount up too much, you can report yourself for general carelessness!

But I was really touched and pleased with the celerity of Your Excellency's re-action. It is clear that you will be a free saint and a Prefect of the City yet. I kiss your hands on it, and I have (more or less) said so in a verse herewith which I could wish were better. But I will blush and point out its faults when you come; take it as a salutation.

Ever,
C. W.

This indeed is measurement, a distance of miles
   Your Excellency covers, faster that you dare see;
this is the first gleam of the sovereign smiles
   that mingle with tears, mourning but mocking, the free
turn in bondage; nay, say more—
   freedom living in bondage; so, she
(sulking in a hole) suddenly herself tore
   herself from the hole and came (with a bruised knee,
gained in the leap), crying 'O infinite fool,
   snorting and snarling; Sir, pay me my fee.
What do they earn who play truant from school
   or negligent slaves? before you speak, I agree.'
I said: 'Nay, look what light shines
   Lois, in you now, through your darkest mines.'

The two letters that follow were his response to what seems to have been a much more comprehensive account of my own experiences than I had previously given him either in writing or when we met. Obviously I was by this time shaping my own image in conformity with what was expected of me. Charles would never have been able to see this. Outright insincerity he would have recognised, on account of its unintelligence: had I been altogether insincere he would not have been interested in me in the first place. What was now happening was that I was being drawn, unconsciously (or *almost* unconsciously, for there was always that glimmer of awareness that eventually grew into a painful comprehension of the truth) into the shining web of Charles's myth.

Southfield House
Oxford
19 Nov./43

This, my dearest girl, is but to acknowledge your writing. I read it at once, and will read it again, and I kiss your hand on it. Saluting with recognition many of the states of mind. O Lois, Lois, have I not almost shrieked in the streets? and walked because I could not sit? and sat because I could not walk? and as for knocking one's head or biting the carpet—!

Yet we have lived by it—and not only *through* it, as fools say—you and I; and under God continue to do so. We; as well as that beatitude of patterned charity which for a moment flashes in us. 'Catch as catch can,' as my Sir Dinadan says. He said something else too which I would look up if I had a *Taliessin;* not having, I content myself with the vague recollection. I will send you, if you haven't got it, and if it's in print, a copy of my *Cranmer of Canterbury;* you might find the Skeleton figure in it of some interest. I wish you had seen it in the Chapter House. Also, if I can find a copy of the script, I will send you a copy of the speech from which that line 'I must unknow . .' came. (It is but the second time so lofty a grace has been allowed me; one of Our children once said she lay during a raid in London repeating *Taliessin* to herself, and holding on so. Leave it; you will believe this is hardly egotism.)

There is nothing to be known but joy: incredible doctrine! Practise, dear and princely heart, the habit of your vows—gently, with laughter, in love. If it amuses you, I will add that I have myself been driven to set in motion an activity to restore (if it may be) to full health a gentleman whose very existence I still a little tend to resent. Mock me, Lois; you are at full liberty; mock me, and go and look at yourself in the glass, and feel a reverberating tenderness of laughter in your ears. You are a fool—but then so am I, and so all. Do you not think He mocked them happily near Emmaus: 'O fools and slow of heart . .' 'O children, children, unimaginable, unutterable *goops!*'

Style, my princess, and always style! 'Love is always courtesy'; 'it does not behave itself unseemly'—that is, its manners are always exquisite. But we have to learn the graces in that sense, as well as Grace in another. I will not offer you—not that you want it . . well, not much!—any more satisfaction than the high Omnipotence permits me. The maddening thing is that satisfaction is there all the time, could one lay hold on it.

You are an (as he said) 'unutterable goop', and a lazybones, and a royalty, and a dear. You are the most slovenly of the slaves and a nun in the convent of Dindrane (called Blanchfleur) where the High Prince Galahad was nursed; indeed you are a foster-warden of the High Prince. You are an inattentive schoolgirl, and you'll probably be caned for inattention during a lesson (indeed, you'd better write out six times that you will be—daydreaming, indeed!). But you are also a serious neophyte and initiate, and an example to Us.

I will write more presently. Meanwhile, continue to be a blessing to me and all Camelot.

C. W.

Southfield House
Oxford
24 Nov./43

And can I raise a *Cranmer* in Oxford? It seems not, and I haven't even a copy of my own. But I hope to do it presently. Meanwhile I send you a typescript of the broadcast play; bring it back when you come. It's not *very* good, but I shall finish one day a half-done Passion play which will (I hope) be better. But you may like to read it. I forget whether we decided you had read *Taliessin?* if not, I'll send it to you. The Lord Palomides was in much our states, on and off.

I turn (how badly I'm writing, but I have always been persecuted by my physical organism; excuse it!) to your History. It may, as you said, be only 'a schoolgirl's exercise'; if so, I can only say that I wish University students would write as sensitively about literature as you about these lordlier Mysteries. I am not, my dearest Lois, paying you compliments; that would be silly. I am, in fact, merely telling you that if you can be so intelligent and clear-eyed and . . and . . and *sound,* I see no chance of your being let off. I am quite serious about this. It's a little difficult to say what I mean without seeming either to pat you on the back or to be talking only of your writing. But your writing is you-at-this-moment, and I don't see why 'unsparing truthfulness' should be kept for blame; I never have. And if, kissing your hand, I were to say that your *History* sparkles with charity and humility and (O celsitudes!) intelligence, why, I might be speaking about someone else, might I not? And we are both passionately agreed that sins co-exist with glories. As much as your giving flowers to Joseph's mother (hypocrisy? heavens, no) with—well, with anything.

I have the profoundest sympathy with him, and I don't think him anything but as much a gem and a jewel as I naturally should. I should have been . . say, I was . . just as incompetent, though for other reasons. And as for your feelings—there is a street in South London I have walked through quicker (almost literally) than the wind because of pain; and the other girl—or the other young man—O Lois, Lois! the rending agony. And even to-day—I would not trust myself, though I think I would a little more trust my own behavior to the Omnipotence. I am a little more capable of believing that It is capable of doing Its own job—even at hell's own crisis if we let it, even in our outer conduct. It is not, in a sense, as you so rightly saw, even we who have to love; undo, undo, and let It.

I think the 'normal human friendship' is sound—only, of course, with all your dedications, and with all that we—try to—believe, it must mean a normal *amicitia* within the Divine City. The very normalities of that state are strange to us. So that there is always the catch. But what then shall I say? I have talked of the Way of Affirmation and the Way of Rejection— yes, but I never separated them at the bottom, and we from moment to moment hardly know which is which; they are but 'categories of one identity'; each in the other, and perhaps especially in these things of human love. It is very urgent that we should practise what is given us as far as we can. I have written—O well, any fool can write (no, but most fools can); but to live it . . ? Yet, under God, there have been moments of fidelity; ask no more; praise, laugh, endure, and be good. It is like your admirable friend's remark on the Song of Solomon; the love poem and the heavenly meaning are one, but we (alas and alas!) have to live them separately.

If (as I think) you have found out some of the diagram; it remains to continue: let me bless you for all that you have done and known. And as for the last 'quarrel'—do not be sad. If he wrote 'very humbly' and you felt 'completely humbled'—dear Lois, what matter? is not that the very nature of the hierarchies? do not let us underrate the condescended beauty. At the end of your life, you will perhaps have only, one way and another, similar things to write; not one, concluding so, but a brick in the City, a vein in the Mystical Body, a word in the great proclaimed Gospel, a Gospel of which all the Rites are but veiled statements. Did you ever read Patmore? but let us rather quote St. Paul: 'Rejoice always; again I say, Rejoice.'

Vow within vow; offer all for him and him to the City. I do believe that this kind of . . offering—I do wish we could find an unspoiled word— finally *works*. Offer yourself to the City, and delicately—as it were, with an air and a grace: manners, always manners!—yourself in the City for him. Become the glory; not that you will notice it if you do. Others may, as I do now, but not you. I am the least of your servants; I am nothing and no one; yet if I say that it remotely gleams on me in your letters, you will not deny it? Prostrate, my Lois, in your room, murmur—well, hardly even murmur; let your heart beat a *Gloria*. It is, we agree, not your doing. But it *is* unique in you, and can only be—so—in you. And that also we believe.

Yes; I think you go on, and go back, and 'watch and pray'. Of course,—do I know the tricks of Omnipotence?!—as soon as you are back, he will be . . O I don't know, moved to Newcastle or made a Bishop or something. We have to move first, and then It does what It chooses. But if you must have sanctity, then sanctity you shall have; that is our true nor- mality. It is most blessed and fortunate that you can see these things and write of them without pompousness, without affectation, without falsity. Yes, I know, I know; it is no credit to you, and you will go and stand in the corner for five minutes, and say to yourself: 'This is for doing my home- work badly', and you may write for me three times: 'Sir, I am the most exquisite dunce that ever lived—but the lesson was a little difficult.' It is no credit to you—no; but you are a credit to it—in a small way, and always under the Protection.

So, ever. We are always expected to have studied the next lesson but one—well, perhaps not, but pass it. I would not have you *too* heavy about day-dreaming; if you find yourself at any one moment seriously inattentive to what has to be done, or ever spending *too* long in reverie treat it as being caught out in a school fault; jump, sigh, smile, and write to me that you were sent up to be punished. It is not worth while that you, who have endured so much rigour with splendour (it seems so; excuse it) should neglect a lesser art. I will have you a shy Glory, and that is all there is to it.

If I have written at all clumsily, excuse that too. I so profoundly believe that the Way is *in* these things—so, and not otherwise, it happens. And if the Way is dim—well, it is.[3] You have done—sinner and fool that you are—very well. Bless you, and again bless you. I will do what I can in my own affairs the better for it. Love—let the web be granite. You will let me know about coming.

C. W.

———————————

Fortunately my head was not turned by all this. I knew that I knew myself better than Charles knew me; and in any case his jugglings with paradox had the effect of depersonalising his comments, depriving them of meaning in any sense that could be applied to oneself. As our correspondence progressed, I was in far less danger of being flattered by Charles than I was of imagining that he was falling in love with me and that I was tremendously important in his life.

It appears from the next letter that I had asked his permission to send the typescript of *The Three Temptations* to the friend who had been the occasion of our meeting and was now providing us with so much to write about. Sadly I reflect that I must have been a sore trial to the poor young man, who had made himself perfectly clear on the subject of our relationship. Charles, however, was not really interested in that relationship as it was in fact, only as he and I were re-creating it in the guise of my "task."

[3] I find that, from the whole of this correspondence, it is this sentence that has impressed itself most deeply on my memory.

Southfield House
31 Nov. [*sic*]/43

At Your Excellency's disposal! send it on by all means. Murmuring perhaps what I said about it; I would not have it thought I rated the poetic value very high. One of these days I will (if so the heavens dispose) give you both lunch; indicate, if you choose, or rather when you choose, the invitation. (You will, no doubt, have considered before now that his name presents you, as it were, to a secret office; the companion of St. Joseph in the august Tale was the Theotokos herself.)

It must be Our lectures at Oxford that have sold what few copies of Our verse Oxford held: *Taliessin* is no more here than Cranmer. But I am promised a copy; it shall be sent when it arrives. If I can find C. S. Lewis's review, you shall read that too. I blush a little at writing so—but how else? You will not think I take credit!

As for coming—if you do me the honour—the sooner the better. I am tied up next Monday and next Wednesday, and possibly Thursday. I would (faintly) rather it next week if it could be managed. But I am also aware that I seem to be imposing both trouble and expense on you, quite without asking you: Let Your Highness's courtesy stretch a hand of pardon. In the Sephirotic tradition, the left side was Severity and the right was Mercy; together they were the Way of Benignity. So, be all things to you; so, all things in you. And to be the means of a peace-offering is more than my own deserts. Or the play's.

Be ever blessed.
C. W.

3 Dec./43

This is only a note to say I have been called to London to-day till Sunday, and on Tuesday owing to the death of my uncle. I shall be back here on Wednesday, and then on. But if you had written and did not get an answer, you might wonder. Let anything you suggest, if anything, after Tuesday, stand.

Ever,
C. W.

Southfield House
6 Dec/43

Admirable! I will meet you in the lounge at the Randolph as near 12.30–12.45 as we can both make it, and we will stimulate ourselves with lunch. I have borrowed *Cranmer* for you.

You do better every day; we will have you a terrible glory yet. See that we talk of your knowledge of literature as well as of sanctity; remember to report yourself for your two lapses; and enjoy being admired.

Ever,
C. W.

After lunching at the Randolph, Charles took me to Southfield House, the temporary headquarters of the Oxford University Press.[4] I had been wondering whether or not he was seriously proposing to carry out the "punishments" he had several times promised to inflict upon me for my various lapses in obedience. The slave girl in the household of the King's poet is lovingly beaten with a hazel rod when she commits a fault; but I was not really expecting this poetic image to be carried over into actual life, until Charles picked up the heavy ruler from his desk and demanded that I should stand before him and hold out the palm of my hand. I did so at once. He struck the palm of my hand with the ruler, courteously and ceremoniously, but hard so that it hurt.

"What have you to say now?" he asked.

I stood quite still and looked him straight in the eyes. "Thank you," I said. I was half angry and totally astonished; but I had no intention of revealing my astonishment. These were his terms. He replaced the ruler and sprang to his feet. A torrent of words poured from his

[4]Anyone who reads my autobiography, *A Time to be Born,* in conjunction with the present book will find a slight discrepancy in the order of events. An episode described in the autobiography as belonging to my second meeting with Charles actually took place at a later date. I suppose this was a slip of memory on my part: in any case, the present account is, I am sure, the correct one.

lips, while he strode about the room, his head jerking
sideways as he talked. Charles, when we were together,
seldom stopped talking; and his speech was so rapid that I
was used to having difficulty in following it; but never had
I seen him like this. More completely even than on the
occasion of our first meeting, I felt stunned with shock. It
was a relief to me when the door opened and Sir Humphrey Milford came into the room. Charles, caught in the
full spate of his daemonic inspiration, presented me, with
a deferential flourish, as to the High King himself. Sir
Humphrey, who loved Charles and must have been used to
it, smiled gently and did not seem at all put out. I was
beginning to realise that even the Oxford University Press
had been compelled to succumb to some extent to the
power of Charles's imposed idea of it.

Before I left Charles gave me a copy of *Paradise Lost,*
setting me the task of reading it and writing an essay on
it. In the years to come I was to look back upon this and
the other literary exercises he set me, as having been the
most real and lastingly valuable part of my "obedience."
Somehow, by the charisma of his personality and the communicated passion of his own devotion to the works of
Shakespeare and Milton—the "divine ones," as he called
them—Charles enabled me to read at least a few of those
works attentively and appreciatively, as if for the first
time. He suspected, he said, that I had been bored with
"doing" them for exams at school: certainly I had ne-
glected to read them since, preferring less substantial
fare, the metaphysicals and the moderns—George Her-
bert, Gerard Hopkins, T. S. Eliot. I was lazy as Charles
often said; but in this respect at least he cured my
laziness.

Southfield House
Oxford
10 Dec/43

It occurred to me yesterday that, if you were reading *Taliessin* on
and off, you might like the typescript of the new poems. I had hoped

they would be out before Christmas, but no! (Apparently the prose note, which you *did* want, is missing; well then, you must wait for that!) My motion towards sending them was confirmed by your letter; I kiss your hand on it. It is partly that we talk the one language; which, for all its commonness, there are so few who do . . without pomposity, without irony, having it written in our flesh. Let us continue; presently the language will spread.

Anyhow, take them for . . O for a Christmas present; or indeed for a small exchange; or indeed for a school prize (but as that, its rather battered condition makes it of a particular kind, suitable and unsuitable at once!). I will perhaps, when you have sent your account of your afternoon at school, turn it into a sonnet—yes?

You were very good and it *was* charming of you to come—as charming as you all through. Next year of course will be stricter. But—when was it you wrote to Us first? How much, how much, since then!

Be ever blessed. 'Be brave, loyal, and fortunate!' And a most joyous Christmas.

C. W.

There was a great deal in the new poems to help me understand what Charles was trying to do—with me, with others, in his verse, and in his personal life. In the poem called *The Founding of the Company*,

On a Sunday, on a feast of All Fools, Dinadan came
to the rose-garden where Taliessin walked. . . .
Dinadan said: 'Well encountered, lieutenant
(they call you) of God's new grace in the streets of Camelot.'
Taliessin answered: 'What should I do, calling
myself a master, and falling so to P'o-l'u?
I should rue the boast there among the marshes,
a lieutenant of the octopods for ever.' Dinadan said:
'Sir, God is the origin and the end God;
cause is comfort and high comfort is cause.
Catch as catch can—but the higher caught in the lower,
the lower in the higher; any buyer of souls
is bought himself by his purchase; take the lieutenancy
for the sake of the shyness the excellent absurdity holds? . . .'

All the same, there were times when I was sorely puzzled, and my apprehension of the "excellent absurdity" gave way to a sense of unfairness. I did not always understand what I was supposed to be doing; and then I felt a fool, not in Charles's meaning of the word but in my own. His next letter refers to such a moment. (The details of my transgression elude me: it had something to do with a "report on my afternoon at school.")

---

22 Dec/43

Nay then—but now—let us begin
with a mere fact; that, temporarily slipping in,
the work arrived.[5] To say only so much
would be perhaps to lose the instinctive touch
that recognizes the Person behind the word
(if the two can be separate). Certainly, I heard
a song . . a song of sealed intention; O
and this before to-day! but now, I know—
more than before? not more than before:
serious in you was the sharp tooth that tore
knowledge into greater knowledge; serious too
the pure will that (yes? yes) would rue
any slipperiness or slowness: is it a small
thing to remark a heart aiming at the all?

Therefore before Christmas I will speak both
laws, Lois: the one against sloth—
the one re-written, joyous, strict,
admired, adhered to; the other—prayer and play;
given a purpose.
    (Do I do anything but speak,
myself? something perhaps; and even the weak
vocation of speech: weak compared to the strong
deed: our iron language does not run along
our lives as acts do; or if—but let be;
it is you we were talking about, and not me.)

Both laws? how *both?* what two
could I mean? the one you first knew,

---

[5]What this means I cannot imagine; but so he wrote it.

discovered, explored, in your heart; and the other growth
that now, as long as it lasts, involves us both.[6]

—but indeed if I am to get this off, I must break off verse and return
to prose, and it would not be decent to leave your letters unacknowledged
till after Christmas, especially being what, and as different as, they are. I
came yesterday by chance on Aquinas on the Transfiguration. He seems to
say that the 'clarity of glory' there seen was the glory which overflows
from His soul into His body; but that with the glorified body this happens
as a permanent quality. 'But in the Transfiguration clarity overflowed from
His Godhead and from his soul into his body, not as an immanent quality
affecting his very body, but rather after the manner of a transient passion,
as when the air is lit up by the sun. Consequently the refulgence, which
appeared then in Christ's body was miraculous.' He adds that the glory of
the soul 'by dispensation might overflow as to the gift of clarity and not as
to that of impassibility.'

You might, *de illo,* like to consider this. I think you must one day
read the theologians. Someone reviewing me once said something about
'the principles' being seen as existing, and certainly the theologians at their
best have that power, and they are a proper accompaniment to the mysteries. I am no Thomist; if I'm anything, it's a Scotist; but Thomas is full of
great definitions. However, there's no hurry. Clarity, chastity, charity—behold the triune laws of the Theotokos and of Your Excellency.

As for your apologies—you are in all things courteous, but I would
not have you 'sad and sorry'. I spoke on the moment—a delicately perfect
moment—and you do nothing but well. Nevertheless, to turn the episode
into laughter, I will see now—writing on—if I can turn it to verse, and if I
do I will have you paraphrase it in prose; a horrid thing they used to be
fond of when we were—when I was young. Like what 'the Bright
Forehead'[7] was. And you too may have done it once, for all I know. Let us
see now—

> Where is your work, Lois? 'Work? . . well
>   I haven't it; you see—' Haven't it? 'No, you see
> I wasn't at all clear . .' You heard me tell

---

[6]This strange outburst illustrates, I think, the way in which, in certain of his states of mind,
Charles's thoughts raced ahead of him, so that even the astonishing rapidity with which he
talked and wrote did not enable him to catch up with them.

[7]"O but the Bright Forehead was once young!" From *The Prayers of the Pope* in *The Region of the Summer Stars.*

> you particularly what—'But then I couldn't be
> quite sure at the moment . .' Come here. 'Besides, to fill,'
>   as she obeyed, 'two pages with so simple a thing
> —could one?' Bring me a cane. She obeyed still.
>   'and I thought I was to wait until my next fling
> of dream.' Hold out your hand. This is grossly unfair?
>   'Grossly.' You were justified? 'Wholly.' But I am right
> now? 'Quite right. I do not suggest you should spare.'
>   Good girl. 'The harder the stick, the higher my flight
> in this air.' She took her stripes; ere the smart could cease,
> she, shining and smiling, was back at her place in peace.

Deign to smile at it . . and begin: 'Lois'—or Lalage, if you like; it is a pleasant name and differentiates . . 'Lalage heard her name called and looked up hastily—'

—O I delay you and yet not unprofitably even so! This will hardly reach you before Christmas; but may after. You *are* a good girl; be ever blessed.

C. W.

I told Charles that Lalage had always been my favorite name. (It has always been one of them.) So I became Lalage. I imagine that he had been casting around for a name to call me, it being his habit to re-christen everyone who was included in his myth. Michal's real name was Florence. He called her Michal after the daughter of Saul who looked out of a window at King David, dancing and playing before the Lord, "and despised him in her heart." Insofar as he loved anyone, Charles loved his wife; but he evidently found her more than a little formidable, and defended himself against her with this kind of whimsical comment on what he supposed to be her attitude towards himself.

Southfield House
1 Jan./44

Thank you for the *Cranmer* and the play. And also for the essay. I've been a little full with speaking here and there, which—by your permission—shall excuse both the delay in this and my not having properly read the essay yet. It was charming of you, though of course only dutiful— quite, quite!—to do your task. If you are as punctual to all virtue, you will do well; in fact you do—in a heavenly sense, we may quote the famous lines from Horace:

Dulce ridemtam Lalagam amabo,
dulce loquentam.

And since he was chronologically before Taliessin, I suppose the King's poet might have seen a manuscript in Byzantium where, no doubt, in the suburbs, he—bought? say so in the Myth—the Greek slave Lalage, whose particular work it was (they say) to see that all the candles in the house were lit at the proper time . . . though sometimes (they also say) she was lazy and lay on her pallet-bed or lounged in the court till the water-clocks had told an hour beyond the proper time; indeed, it is even said that occasionally the Lord Taliessin, wishing to write verse, found his own room dark—after which (as might be expected) Lalage spent some time in general discomfort, though no one lost any joy. However. . .

There is a thing you might do for me. One of Our people is returning from Bermuda—'the still-vexed Bermoothes'—to England. She has her child with her, and will very much hate the voyage; her husband has asked me to do what I can. And it occurred to Us that, in this matter, you were pre-designed by Almighty God to be of use to God, to Us, and to Our household. The journey, I imagine, will take about three weeks. It is, of course, in these circumstances, impossible to make any compact of exchange. But it is likely she will believe that We and the Company will do anything that can be done. And We lay it in your hands. You will therefore, without anxiety and in tranquility, pray for her and present yourself shyly to Almighty God in exchange for her. If nothing whatever happens you will not be surprised; if you are, one way or another, suddenly inconvenienced, you will not be surprised. This is a real thing, and you will do it handsomely and even gaily—without fancy or invention—for the Company and the Doctrine. Her name in this world is Alice Mary; the second of these may be in the Union. (Though she was, once, of a remarkably different type; a very sinful and very noble creature. But not—I do but breathe it for clarity's sake—my own Lady of the Window.)[8]

---

[8]Charles often referred to Phillida (or Celia) in this way. The reference is, of course, to Dante. Michal was his "Beatrice" because she came first in time; although his case differed

I have another point in mind for you when this is done. But for the next three weeks, Lalage, We commit it to your charge. As if, for that time, you lit the candles on the altar for this particular thing.

Be ever blessed,
C. W.

Charles talked and wrote a great deal about the practice of "exchange." It was one of the root rules of the Company. One made a pact and picked up the other person's fear or grief or pain and carried it oneself. This was the theory at any rate. The trouble was that, while the theory was irrefutable, the practice was apt to be dubious. In the case of Alice Mary, I did not really understand exactly what I had to do. I could pray for her, of course. But *how*, I asked myself, was I to "present myself shyly to Almighty God in exchange for her"? And, for that matter, whispered a still small voice at the bottom of my heart, why *should* I, just because Charles said so? Alice Mary was in real danger, voyaging across mined seas in time of war. Was I seriously being asked to suffer all that daily fear, including perhaps the terror of an actual disaster, without Charles having had the least reason to suppose that I was inwardly prepared and willing to do anything of the sort? Because if that was not what it meant, it meant nothing. It was moral blackmail. I knew this; but I could not bear to know it; and so I dismissed the idea, and turned my attention to carrying out my task. I prayed for Alice Mary, adding a half-hearted codicil to the effect that here I was.

Meanwhile, it seems that I was moved by an anniversary associated with my own love-affair, to reopen the subject.

from Dante's in that his second Lady aroused in him the greater passion and was the inspiration of his mature verse.

Southfield House
7 Jan./44

Yes. Though with anyone else I should, I think, considerably modify that blank statement by adding (i) that he will only love as *he* can love (ii) that any real charity is apt to seem like granite to us (iii) that it is, sooner or later, necessary that we shall abandon the last hope. But these things will have been clear to you, and I certainly will never deny that beyond the impersonalities the personalities return. It's almost impossible—I do not say quite—to demand nothing for oneself; not to desire even the mere personal consciousness that love is returned. There, most sweetly, most delicately, most subtly, lies 'the old man on the new way'. Eliot, in his essay on Dante, speaks of 'a renunciation of feelings that persist beyond the grave'. The co-inherence of that renunciation with the theological assertion, of the theological assertion with the renunciation—this is the Way. Not (if you will forgive me) 'since you so love him'—he can only love you because God loves you. He must 'somewhere, somehow in the City'—love you? yes; but it will be, O princess, the other side of Lear's 'Never, never, never, never, never.' The first time one says 'never' is almost appalling; so is the first time one seriously thinks of being loved only—*only*—because God loves. The air is rarefied. Yet I suspect you are wise enough to breathe in it. Charity demands charity—yes; but (in a sense) only of charity.

Nevertheless, let the blessings be with you for Sunday in the Octave. Believe that that was holy and happy in the instant when it happened; if you can, I shall be surprised: can I? I doubt it; yet unless so, I do not believe at all. You have lived yourself partly by his word; it was that which remained faithful to you in your worst times—yes? But this is the other way round? yes; he (sent by the other He) came 'to turn the world upside down'. That is why, so often, 'unselfish' and 'selfish' are words that mean sometimes each other in the end—that is a rash comment; modify as Your Intelligence sees.

I send you a set of proofs of the Introduction to the Underhill letters: for one reason chiefly—the chat about the Impossibility may interest you. On p. 26, though the sentence was first written before your first letter 'the fidelity and the labour' might have been written for you. But fourteen years?[9] It is eighteen since my own small Impossibility began. It is not now

---

[9] "Fourteen" refers to Evelyn Underhill, not to me. Charles is suggesting that I had only just begun.

very present, for various reasons, but . . . ? O Lalage, the same business house is no easier than the same town: impossibility of repose, impossibility of escape: blessings without number and a curse intertwined with all. Mad ness and pain and horror—and inexorable beauty still. I will give you a Celia for your Joseph. One day—no, you are not likely to meet her, and she would be to you—'who,' said my son when he was at Blackwell's one day, 'was the middle-aged woman in a beret with Sir Humphrey?' Only she who was Shekinah when he was just one year old—and you were six; no, I err: he was three and you were eight. And now? We grow old, but the Doctrine lives. Exalted for ever be the Mercy of the Omnipotence!

Well . . Milton. I should like you to write what *you* think about it as a poem. Just as a poem. Chat about it; tell me any lines you liked and any bits you thought dull. Be at ease with it; poetry is to be enjoyed. I allow I pontificated a little,[10] but so do not you; there was a cause for mine. Take a large number of risks, and dance.

And as for being fidgeted—all the gods in their sacred synod, and all the It which is They, forbid! It is exactly what I would not have you be. I would rather you forgot all the accidents—well, *almost* rather. But I think your own idea preferable; do it so till Easter, and then let us consider it again; then you will not feel hideously bound to one mode for ever. You are a good girl, Lalage; besides being—all the other things, and next time you write, add a P.S. saying so. A handsomely honest creature, and worth dis- covery. Though, of course, insufferable.

> Blessings. In general and on this Feast.
>
> Ever,
>
> C. W.

> Did I know in my heart even then that what Charles was calling "the fidelity and the labour" could at least equally well have been described as a form of self-indulgence? I had learnt, and was still learning, hard and valuable les- sons from my abortive love-affair: one of them would prove to be that one can actually enjoy being miserable and seek to prolong one's unhappiness when it makes one seem interesting to oneself. Charles was totally oblivious

---

[10]In his Introduction to the O.U.P. "World's Classics" edition.

of this kind of psychological motivation. In the same way he disregarded the psychological aspect of the experience of falling in love: he could not see that the aura of "glory" surrounding the beloved is largely self-induced, and is in any case very seldom, if ever, the result of a direct perception of the particular individual as he or she is existing in the heavenly state. (Only once in my life, and that in my schooldays, have I experienced a "falling in love" so pure and radiant that it does indeed seem, in retrospect, to have been a communication from a higher realm: even that, however, had little to do with the person as she was in herself.)

Meanwhile Charles expected me to report to him every time I was bad tempered towards my mother; and I scrupulously did so.

Southfield House
7 Jan./44

Your letter came just after I had sealed mine; and as I go to London for the week-end, and do not wish you to think I delay over such points of high courtesy (I mean yours rather than mine) I permit myself to answer at once. But since it pleased the Omnipotence unusually to hold me still—I mean, in that sense of momentary fixedness—after the Eucharist yesterday, and since your note came on the Feast—why, let us be gentle and debonair—not that you are not always debonair—but I will have you, if there is any pleasant word or phrase you use sometimes to your mother, or some lightness or tenderness of gesture, to use it once particularly because of you in Us and in the Empire,[11] and I so in You and the Empire. And when you are here again you shall give me, Lalage, your hand to be kissed, as Dindrane might, and afterwards you shall kiss mine, but that I think on a knee, ceremonially. And this is an order and you will remember it.

For what should those of Carbonek do sometimes but practise the substance of ceremony?

Blessings,
C. W.

---

[11]Byzantium.

I sometimes venture to think I was a little good for
Charles. In the midst of confessions of bad temper, ex-
changes with Alice Mary, essays on Milton, and rarefied
exercises in the ways of romantic love, I firmly requested
him to "carry" for me my trepidation at the prospect of
conducting the Sunday school in Thaxted church.

Southfield House
Oxford
11 Jan/44

Having sent off my note to you, I shot up to London, but (oddly
enough, as it seems) you and it remained a little on my mind. I thought that
what I wrote was proper, once—and then—but I also thought that in a
general way, for these domestic snarlings, you needed something quite different. And when I returned to find your second admission, I was con-
vinced of it. What you need, Lalage, every time you go on like this, is a
sound thrashing at once, and if you lived nearer you should have it. As it is,
you will when you come next, and you had better be very careful indeed
how you run to three times before you *do* come. These particular kinds of
irritation are especially difficult to deal with 'spiritually' as one may say—
it is something in the very relationship that excerbates the nerves. A little
'servile fear', my angel, will do you no harm. I would not use it unless you
had a royalty. And meanwhile you will be good enough to copy out for me
the speech of Satan in *Paradise Lost* IV. 32–113; remembering that it is a
great moment of choice and (it is an order) considering this time the great
poetry as well as the religion; and you will add a nine-times-copied sentence foretelling your thrashing.

—Your letter has just come, and because I will 'hurry', I will not
stop to answer it in full. February certainly—as early as you choose: that
leaves you only three weeks to be happily scared—if I may so put it. But I
hope the happiness will be there and act as well as the scaring—not that
scaring is the right word: excuse! But observe how right you are—you are
more equal, even the more sovereign, the more you are . . abased? well,
say so: it is not quite right, but pass. It is, I think, something of this that
lies in the dark saying about taking the lowest seat and being in that called
up higher. I have the beginning of a poem somewhere on those lines.

As for Sunday . . . I will certainly lay myself open to . . why, let us say being scared again! And you will leave it to me. O I assure you that even naturally, I should be—with children, and indeed am a little already. So you need not, and will not, be distressed; and each time you write your nine times sentence, you will leave the other to me. A very happy and fortunate arrangement—of which both you and I on the one hand, and on the other your mother and the children derive the benefits. And if you say that you, in the end, will pay for all . . why not, my Lalage, and again how fortunate! If you think so. (Or if you don't.)

I am a little taken with your interpretations. Of course you are right about Charity, and about the rest, I think, but I will take longer to think. The Church and Nature, in some sense must be one; behold the City!—but of that another time. Your Excellency's dispositions are noble: you *are* a good girl. And you will leave Sunday to God and Us.

Be blessed.
C. W.

Southfield House
19 Jan/44

Yes, you will be, for all I know, thinking I am 'shocked' and I know not what if I delay so long. But I hoped you would let me know about Sunday, and lingered, and then yesterday . . . O well, this will reach you before the week-end!

I am very glad about Sunday. It was most right of you to ask, and you will do so at any similar time. It was no inconvenience; something of a depression for most of the day, which (since I chose—properly, I think—to locate it with you) was even agreeable. It is, you see, your bounden duty to do the best you can for the babies, and if this is the best? Continue, princely lady; you shall have style—our beloved style—in everything.

Whatever you do, I shan't think you don't care. Considering what human nature is like, I could bear to whisper to you that I don't think you do too badly . . but hush! or you will think I am not taking you seriously, which I should hate. There is a kind of unintentional symbolism in P'o-l'u being in the feet, as it were; we wander about, and the deliberate effort at control is almost (as we all know) as deadly as no effort—at least in its effects. Observe people being self-denying and the dire results! I have no idea of your being tiresome in religion. (Someone remarked the other day that my great title to . . O to whatever was that I had taught a few people how *not* to believe in the Faith. Ascribed to the only Omnipotence . . and so forth; but there is a grain of truth in it.) You are to be my own princess. Day-dreams are a perfect pest, I know; do I know! they catch and tangle— well, they do! You shall tie a piece of cord or string or something round your left ankle for the next seven nights when you go to bed—not too tight; I don't want you kept awake from checking the blood-flow—as a deed done (after all if slaves will dither, they must expect to be chained!), but with (by Your Excellency's permission) a smile, and perhaps even another when you take it off in the morning? And you will let me know that you will have your ears boxed, with every kind of sympathy!!

As for your mother, I know exactly. Why—WHY, dear Lalage, does one start arguments when one knows what will happen? But we have discussed that, or rather we've settled about you. (It's up to you, you know, to keep me up to it—a little. There is a certain courage demanded, and you— it may or may not surprise you to know—for all your docility have a certain lioness-effect calculated to scare most . . . Masters? Let me blush and use the word.)

I shall certainly be here on the 15th., because I lecture at 11 that day. But perhaps another—perhaps the Thursday would give us more leisure. There is a faint chance that Dorothy Sayers may choose that day to come and discuss things at the Press, which would spoil things. But I shall know (I hope) in a week or so. Meanwhile let us provisionally fix on the Thursday, the 19th.

I repeat, Lalage, I have the greatest admiration combined with the most brutal intentions. What could a fledgeling saint ask more?

C. W.

You always were getting better. But I love to think that I am any help.

24 Jan./44

And now to write you a line before I do anything else. Thank you for the *Dublin*. And thank you for your Milton. I propose, as soon as I get a chance, to read it to C. S. L.: he will be delighted. When you come, remind me to lend you his book on M. The charming thing is that you have said exactly what he said about Satan—or almost. He points out that Satan has only one subject in every speech. And your own comment gallops in twin harness with that. (It's all very well for Lewis; but when it comes to a schoolgirl like Lalage in her English literature lesson saying something I ought to have remarked and did not, I'm not at all sure that it isn't—well, not impertinence, for, of course, it's pertinent enough, but something like cheek. However . . .)

I should think you must be one of a very few to react to the divine Milton in this admirable way. But our academic schools have ruined him for us. I agree also about what you say on the Adam-Eve relationship. Milton in prose on husbands and wives is apt to jarr considerably. The poor lamb was perhaps unfortunate; still . . but he does almost wholly get away with it here; and in an unfallen state . . . Though even there Eve had her 'sweet austere composure'—it is in Book IX; a perfect passage. Adam has been putting it over her; and she replies with that horrid chill in her voice which all men are terrified by in their ladies; and he (1. 290) hastily soothes her down:

> To whom with *healing* words Adam replied,
> Daughter of God and Man, immortal Eve . . .

'Healing'! I'll say so. You will observe also in her speech that, though she's let the poor boob think he's telling her something, she's taken care—by accident—to know all about it first; and now she lets him know he was quite superfluous with all his information—

> *both* by thee informed I learn
> And from the parting angel overheard

O Milton knew more than he knew he knew about glorious and divine ladies. But while we think him portentous, we shall never see it.

I should rather like you now to read some Shakespeare; also my own *English Poetic Mind*, but the second can wait. I lecture on *Othello* tomorrow; then on *Lear* next week, and *Macbeth* the week after; and *Antony* next. (I must have got muddled in my dates—Thursday is the 19th Feb., I see.) I think you might keep alongside. But first look up the speech in *Troilus and Cressida* which is the very definition of all such crises—V. ii. 134.[12] I don't mean we all go through exactly . . . O but I forgot; I said all this in

---

[12]"Nothing at all, unless that this were she. . . ." This line and the speech that follows were frequently quoted by Charles, as illustrating the contradictions between the "two aspects" of the beloved, and the Impossibility that is nevertheless a fact.

the *Figure of Beatrice;* well, look it up, considering poetry and its exquisite accuracy; and then go on to *Othello*. Read it with the fresh and undimmed eyes you brought to Milton. You are a princely creature, and you have an intelligence equal to your years. Which (considering mankind) is really a high compliment.

Alice Mary has arrived safely, I hear; so you are free from that business. Of the other I had in mind we will speak; meanwhile you might merely open, as it were, the particular intentions of certain healings within the Company to our Lord the Spirit. Without stress and in shy faith. It will serve till I see you. The Taliessin poems delay their publication, but you shall have a copy, of course, as soon as they do get out. And thank you for liking them (yes? yes).

I kiss your hand. Be ever a glory.

C. W.

I will add a thank you . . much of our conversation consists in 'thank you'; sweet! . . for your latest promise. Pardon, authority—even punishment—are all in some sense *mutual* acts. Precisely in so far as they are not frankly encouraged as mutual (I agree, of course, they cannot always be!), they do not possess their true nature. I am sure this is true of very much; here also is the grand equality—for the offices (so to call them!) are equal, in whatever the offices consist. Besides the souls. And I will send you a stamp for your next letter in exchange.

I am sometimes asked how fond I think Charles really was of Lewis (who adored him, to the exasperation of Tolkien, who did not); and to what extent he felt identified with the group calling themselves "the Inklings," who used to meet in an Oxford pub and talk about their work. The only honest answer is that I have no idea. But I have a suspicion that Charles, in this context, enjoyed being stimulated to talk, while inwardly distancing himself from those to whom he talked. Perhaps, too, he enjoyed seeing himself, occasionally, as a man amongst men. This is, after all, one aspect of the romantic ideal.

Southfield House
25 Jan./44

(Your postman will weave dreams about these embossed envelopes—
'tis your problem!)[13]

This is but a note to say that I have done as I said. In a pub next door
to Mr. Blackwell's famous bookshop, I read to Mr. C. S. Lewis (Fellow of
Magdalen), to Mr. J. R. R. Tolkien (Bosworth Professor of Anglo-Saxon),
and to Major Lewis (C. S. L.'s brother), your comments on Milton. Omit-
ting, by some trick of decision, the phrases 'you gave me to write out' and
'making me read it'—why? you will know as well as I.

Anyhow they all approved highly—not that I trust any of their judgements, but CSL's, on Milton—and said how intelligent you were—which is
true—and how well it was put—which is not necessarily so true; and CSL
even went so far as to say he would like to see you, and I have promised
that perhaps one day he shall; we will see how it can be worked. And you
have got over extremely well, and I am properly pleased, but more inclined
to think it cheek of you than ever. For what is all this clarity? did you not
say you were a goop? and did I—or did I not—agree? and here you are
approved . . bah!

> Lalage said: 'I wrote something today
>   which was approved by the great. I knew at once
> that I should (most unfairly) have to pay
>   for attributed insolence. "What, you, my dunce,"
> —and so on . . and perhaps stand on the form, or write
>   a thousand lines, or even be caned on my hands,
> or what not. Indeed, it seems a pretty plight
>   when one cannot succeed, when one cannot obey commands,
> without trouble! after all, I wrote what I thought—
>   and really one's master should be gratified at sense;
> and I wondered if I should say so; I felt I ought,
>   and yet I felt somehow that any defence
> would be . . injudicious. I thought . . "No;
> perhaps there is some sense in its happening so." '

Anyhow you had better go and stand in the corner with your hands
behind you till you have counted twenty—

---

[13]Charles always used O.U.P. envelopes in writing to me.

No; but, seriously, you will know I was pleased, and you will be a little pleased yourself at the fantasy. Deign to permit the dance of comment—yes?

C. W.

I had written to Charles about my brother who died, not long after I was born, at the age of sixteen. This brother was my only sibling. His was, by all accounts, a rare soul: I thought about him a great deal, and believed in the existence of a spiritual bond between him and myself.

Southfield House
3 Feb./44

You will think I am neglecting you, but I hope it is not so. I have been in London and then rushed with tutorials and things. Pass, and pardon.

I have tried to find in the *New Christian Year*—yes; I know, and I am conscious of a failure in not sending it (if it is still in print)—We will try and get a copy on the 19th. and anyhow you will ask me for a shilling in token of your own hierarchical rights; and I hope you get it! but you will demand it anyhow; it is as much an order as any of the other kind—a quotation from the (no doubt) Blessed St. Seraphim of Sarov, who (I seem to remember) caused one of his followers to die in place of her brother in order that he might do some other job. It was perhaps a little extreme of Seraphim, and I should not care to do it myself, but then I am certainly no saint, and most certainly no Russian saint. But you will see how it came into my mind. And I think two things— (i) Without dictating to the Omnipotence, I think you may (what paper! well, it can't be helped) reasonably feel precisely what you do feel. If (in some sense) he lives for you among the Celestials, even if almost, as it were impersonally, still for you impersonally (it is too crude a word, but you will know what I mean) then certainly you may very well live his life on earth . . . 'dying each other's life, living each other's death.' I would almost say that if you choose to have it so, then so it shall be. And, if it were not presumptuous, I would almost add that, 'by the authority committed to Us,' and in the virtue of Our absurd lieutenancy, We ratify and seal your thoughts and intentions so:

always remembering, of course, that the acts will be yours in kind; but some mutual, such as your talking to children.

(ii) The *N.C. Year* had a quotation from a book of the hermits of the Thebaid, called *The Paradise of the Fathers*, which says: 'Keep they conscience with thy brother, and thou shalt find rest.' Of course, brother there means . . I know; still an actual brother is also a brother in the other sense, and it seemed to me a very proper and suitable saying for you. And so, as you have no doubt already seen, with any great phrase that uses the word, always with care and always with style; modesty in magnificence, magnificence in modesty; scepticism in faith, faith in scepticism. Take the particular application with a smile, a private salutation, a kiss and a wave of the hand in the City: in fact you might throw your brother a light kiss on the very phrase I quoted . . . yes, actually, now; your fingers, Excellency, to your lips, cast it into the air, and so God take all!

('It would,' said I once to the Lady of the Window, with some general reference to her own secret life, 'have happened anyway, I there or no.' 'Yes,' said she, 'all I'm asking you to get into your thick head is that it *did* happen this way.')

You are not, Lalage, nearly as much like a goop as it pleases Your Highness to say. And there isn't the slightest danger of my thinking that you think yourself Somebody. I may be permitted to have a slight tendency to admire you myself, for various reasons: for what? O I don't know— *Othello* . . . substitution . . . frankness of honour . . virtue . . even (hush! in your ear) gaiety . . religion. I allow of course the catterwauls [*sic*] and the claws; but still . . let us try one more verse—

> Someone said: 'What are you doing there,
>   Lalage, in the hall? what light do you hold?'
> She looked at the candle held at the level of her fair
>   smile; she answered: 'Nay, it were much too bold
> to say *It is I;* did I not have to keep
>   my leg fettered for not polishing the swords?
> and indeed (to be honest) I barely sprang from sleep
>   in time to hold this for the Progress of the Lords
> to the King's table; but they say . . . the Lord Taliessin says
>   this is as much myself as the self I know,
> though I burn as deeply red as this candle's blaze
>   bright, at the thought; I wait till the Lords go,
>   or the High Prince come, in a lighting of the time;
>   and my Lord Taliessin this morning turned a rhyme.'

I can't think how you manage to read the divine ones—meaning the poets—so *freshly.* Did you never go to school? Did you never do literature there? Or were you always, without the present-day consequences, inattentive? Or what? It is almost unusual. I will discuss *Othello* another time, but I quite definitely liked your chat. You must read CSL's *Allegory of Love*—a great book on European poetry from Rome to Spenser: you might, I think, like it. Dorothy Sayers is coming next week; she will not interfere with us. As for husbands and wives—another time; it is certainly a changing hierarchy, and perhaps the only real difference in their separate obediences is that it is somehow suitable that the femininity should speak it aloud! I will write your name in your hand for your own speech of your—punishment? leave the dancing word; hold me to that too. Be blessed.

C. W.

Your document has just arrived. Child, do I know these refuges? they may even be better than worse; so, as you say, let us even in tiresomeness, try and smile. You shall forget them when (even) you

flatter the mountain tops with glorious eye.

8 Feb/44

Of course you are right, and I am . . . as near a goop as our Magnificence can allow itself to be: Thursday is the 17th. I will come to the Randolph as near 12 as I can: you will be there by then, and we will lunch there before, and probably come on here afterwards; we could borrow a room there, but the myth (so to speak!) has always treated the Press as near Byzantium in its own way.

If the least of your servants may say so, I shouldn't call your last report too bad? I put the question mark in very hastily, so that you may not think I'm glozing or anything. Still, even rabbits may be admired? And if rabbits, why not slaves? And if slaves, why not Dindrane? . . . Sister of Percivale, and all that? O I would not say but what the star of Percivale hadn't something to do with you: it is, after all, better *not* to seem bad-tempered than to seem. By next Advent you shall seem good-tempered, even if it is only the star-shine on the subtleness of Your Excellency's blood. Or if stars do not shine much on rivers, and perhaps they do not, why, call it the sun at once—and do you, visualising sunlight on a strong river, say seven glorias for the fantasy of that creation, shyly believing.

I was impressed by what you said about Othello, especially about the death of Iago, which last night I handed on to one of my pupils, nobly saying that it was someone else's idea. I have remarked somewhere that Shakespeare is incredibly capable of describing supernatural states in natural terms; it is dangerous to say so because the religious people are always trying to annex him—no; not you; you were quite right in all you said about morality; but we do not advance religion by false criticism, and so many of the pious seem to think we do. But in *Othello*—

O the labours of this world interrupted me! and here is your letter of *Lear* before I have dealt with *Othello,* but I will catch up, though not now, for I must go and find Miss Sayers, who is a nice creature, and is always kind to my own literary efforts. No, Lalage, that is NOT a feline scratch; it is a Dove's wing jest. She *is;* and so am I to hers. But that, of course, is DIFFERENT.

For the rest—I am glad you cheered yourself up! I am precisely glad we can laugh over it. You are not, by a miracle, being tiresome or troublesome. And you are being gay and debonair. But Wentworth went to hell because of the denial of the Guard's shoulder knots, and because he envied, hated and denied Aston Moffatt. Otherwise he might have been free from all—even ghostly succubi! They are as much our unhappy fate as anything else. It is the other thing which damns us.

I kiss your hands. Be always Lalage.

C. W.

I travelled to Oxford this third time in a painfully divided state. On the one hand, I adored Charles. I believed myself to be in love with him: in any case, my former love, however I might use it as a means of keeping his attention and collecting his elaborate compliments, had been almost ousted from my thoughts by Charles himself. On the other hand, I was very slightly resentful and very much perplexed. A sense of unreality, which had never been altogether absent from my mind in connection with my "obedience," was becoming more insistent. I realised that Charles had manoeuvered me into a position where I could not refuse him anything without seeming to refuse him ev-

erything. This in itself was a kind of trap. To compound
my problems, the stream of paradox whereby Charles defined the nature of our relationship, by making his behaviour theoretically unassailable, in practice made his
dominion over me complete. I could accuse him of nothing.
Had I complained that he was treating me like a slave he
would have kissed my hand and called me a princess. Had
I murmured that perhaps it was not altogether reasonable
to expect me to be constantly writing out lines, standing in
corners, and tying up my ankles with bits of string, he
would have agreed with me at once. Had he not repeatedly
said the same? And in any case, of course, I had no intention of suggesting to him any such things. I understood
very well that the mythological structure within which
Charles had enclosed me was a perfect globe, a bubble
that must not be pricked at any point. Within that enclo-
sure I possessed him—or I felt that I did—in a particular
manner that, bewildering as it might be, was none the less
delectable and, at that time, more important to me than
anything else in my life. I accepted his terms. Only I
could not help noticing that those terms had been wholly,
down to the minutest detail, dictated by him: there was
nothing mutual about them, for all his talk of mutuality.

The immediate question was what precisely he was going to do about my "punishment." I could not believe
that he was really intending to carry out his promise to
"thrash" me. But when we were alone together in his
room at Southfield House, after I had kissed his hand,
kneeling on one knee, and he had kissed mine, he told me
to bend over a chair and lift up my skirt. When I did so,
he took the ruler and struck me hard on the behind. I
stood up, feeling bruised in more senses than one. Charles
was walking about the room, as he had done on the pre-
vious occasion, talking as if he were agonisedly trying to
catch up with ideas that were forever flying beyond his
reach. Suddenly he paused in front of me and, putting his
arms about me, held me close to him in a strange stillness, a silence that could not have been more unlike his
usual excitement. I stayed still and scarcely breathed.
Charles had shown no sign of being sexually aroused at

any time; nor did he seem to be now. I could not imagine what he wanted of me.

Since then I have come gradually to a partial understanding of what it was that Charles was trying to do. Somewhere on the borderlines of religion and magic there exists a traditional methodology concerned with the achievement of power through sexual transcendence. This idea is not—or not necessarily—a part of the cult of romantic love in the Dantean sense, although there is clearly a strong association between the two. The practitioner enters into intimate physical contact with a woman (or man where the orientation is homosexual) without sexual arousal taking place beyond a certain predetermined point. (In Hindu and Buddhist Tantra this point is almost incredibly far advanced, resulting in what seem to us bizarre practices of supreme restraint and sexual acrobatics.) In the Middle Ages the cult of love sometimes involved sleeping naked by the side of a naked woman with an unsheathed sword between. The two methods—typified by the Beatrician ideal on the one hand, and Tantric exercises on the other—together exemplify the way in which apparent opposites can become, in practice, inextricably entwined. At the highest level of all, where the goal sought is the state of unification with Divine Love, the theme blends imperceptibly into the mysticism of the Sufis and the flowery ecstasies of a John of the Cross. I am wholly unqualified to say more: but this much must be said, if one is to begin to understand the kind of relationships with young women that Charles, whose fascination with this particular tradition, in all the forms it has assumed in the West, was second only to Christianity as a dominant influence in his life, was in the habit of setting up. He once confessed (not to me) that his work demanded these practices: only so could his creative powers be released. No doubt this was true; but it was surely only part of the truth. I believe that, from some cause inacessible to the understanding of his friends, Charles had become addicted to this strange form of intoxication: he needed to wind himself up into the utmost state of tension of which he was capable, and then to relax into stillness—as he did when he took me in his arms and held me in silence. He died in his fifties because his nervous energies and his physical frame were utterly exhausted by the stresses he imposed upon himself.

He imposed also considerable stresses upon the chosen partners of these experiments. I returned to Thaxted in a state of dangerous exhaustion, and almost immediately became seriously ill. Even so, it appears, from his next letter, that I wrote to him immediately, protesting that my punishment had been inadequate. I could do this almost without being conscious of insincerity, because it was imposed upon me by my role. What my role prescribed for me became—or seemed to become—while the play lasted, something that I *had to do*.

---

22 Feb./44

Handsomely done! was (I confess) what I was going to say, had I written first, and will still. It is (you will have observed) one thing to have views, and another to act conformably. But you did both; and you may have been right that I was not quite as handsome (so to call it) as you deserved and had a right to expect. Attribute it partly to time and place—place because these walls are thin and one can be overheard; time because I was not sure how far Your Excellency was prepared . . No, no insult; no doubt; call it an 'inevitable ceremony of approach'. But do not think that I seriously hesitate. If you ever have to be whipped again—and I would not altogether put it past you—I shall borrow a room, and you will have six particular stripes before that whipping. And so God 'ild Your Excellency! It is a punishment, a game, and a shaping; and I will play my part with more rigour now I have seen with what freshness of truth you play yours. As for your account, it was gay and charming and something more. But O alas! I would be of no use if . . .

They only can do it with my lord who can do it without him.

I must be a great poet—I'm so accurate in verse. Which reminds me that I feel I owe you a sonnet, but yesterday's lecture, tutorial, novel,[14] and

---

[14]*All Hallows Eve.*

air-raid duty have left me stale—O nonsense, I must try—on another sheet: and you shall forgive more to-day.

Except that you must, I think, now read some theology—*real* theology. I see there is a translation of St. Anthanasius *On the Incarnation* just out; which I want. When I have it, I'll lend it to you.

And so all blessings. And thank *you*.

C. W.

> Lalage, having with propriety turned her skirt,
>   and conveniently thrown herself forward against a chair
> (*proporio motu*) said: 'It didn't hurt
>   as my dues demanded.' Be then, Fair,
> content to let your honourable openness pay
>   those dues this once; laugh deep in your heart,
> to find the mere gesture decked the day
>   with completeness; and leave to another the better smart.
> So neither shall my courtesy be then spared
>   nor this of yours lost; ask meanwhile
> for any that becomes us. O having well fared
>   these six months, be ever-proved in a larger style.
> 'Gay, intelligent, holy'—rise and shine
> everywhere; as here . . being here not undivine.

Southfield House
3 March/44

I had meant to write earlier, but things defeated me: you are never to suppose, if there is a delay, that I have not attended to you. And indeed I wished—but too ineffectively—to soothe, so to speak, your distressed hours. Which, I hope, are for the time over.

In a sense your epigram about marriage and my Taliessin line both might indicate, I suppose, a certain belief? or at any rate a willingness towards a belief in something beyond the Derivations of which we talk? Of course, it might, I quite see, be mere pride . . but you needn't start exercising yourself about that! The fantasy of finding oneself saying one's life has been blessed when one looks back on the glooms and agonies—not wholly perhaps one's own fault—is odd enough to keep Your Highness's humility occupied for some time. And, as far as can be, let your Highness live from the nature of that beatitude.

The difference between that looking forward, past the undesirable moment, to putting everything right again, and not allowing (as far as one can) the moment, is, I suppose, something of the difference between the old man on the new way and the new man on the new way. And it takes some time to make the substitution. At the same time, it will be apparent to you that the result of such postponements would be, if pursued, to justify them. And then, as I hinted to you, there would be a moment at which I shouldn't punish you; there would be no point and no profit. Be wholly at ease now; I do but adumbrate a possibility which is far enough. One day you must be free, but I would rather it were by your outstripping all than by my desisting merely.

At the same time (excluding your worse time) it doesn't seem too bad a month, and I entertain a faint belief that, say a year ago, Lalage, you would hardly have believed it could happen so well; in the normal course of things and plus the staying in bed. Though in the future, when you have to stay in bed, you will be good enough to regard it as being confined to your prison in the King's poet's household, at Our will, for what negligences you may have inconvenienced the house by commiting. So accepting it, with some gloom, but debonairly.

And as for all, what you will do, my Lalage, is to learn by heart the overthrow of the rebel angels in *Paradise Lost,* Book VI, line 824 to 912, which is 89 lines in all; and when you come next, you will say them to me, and you will get a cut on each hand whenever you make a mistake. And when your master gave you that imposition one afternoon in school, and your (imaginary) neighbour whispered to you 'That's very unfair!' you will tell me what you whispered back and how you were immediately given four cuts for talking.

Be ever blessed.

C. W.

I was by this time too weak to get across the room without my mother's help. I could hardly lift a knife and fork; but still I contrived, with what labour he never knew, to write to Charles. My condition went unexplained. It was almost certainly (I realise now) an acute manifestation of an illness I have had all my life as the result of a virus infection in childhood: on the other hand, I have no doubt that its immediate cause was to be found in the stresses imposed upon me by my relationship with Charles. I lay in bed for six weeks; and there was no question of my doing any "exercises," literary or otherwise. When Charles realised this, he was instantly, eagerly, accommodating and kind. How was it then that I sensed an almost imperceptible withdrawal behind the kindness? I knew that I was letting him down. I knew too that I should be able to reinstate myself completely the moment I was sufficiently recovered to resume my "obedience." He was only waiting for this: and so (except that I did not feel as if I should ever recover) was I. Or so I supposed, being far too exhausted to face the possibility of any other choice.

Meanwhile I was attempting, half-consciously, for the first time, to impose my own terms upon our correspondence; I asked some rather academic questions about numerology; and I sent Charles the typescript of a book I had written, some years previously, for children, ostensibly with the idea of his reading it for the Press. Small enough departures from pure role-playing, one would think. And yet, through the haze of sickness, I was aware of dangers. My devotion to Charles was undiminished. Propped up with pillows, I was reading the "Celia" poems, a bundle of which I had brought back with me from Oxford, and they were not improving my spirits. As poetry, I thought them superior to the *Taliessin* cycle, which I could not admire because I found most of it incomprehensible. But my feelings were lacerated by the communicated anguish. Moreover I was jealous. It was a blessed relief to turn altogether from thoughts of Charles to the novels of the anonymous author of *Elizabeth and her German Garden*, a set of which had been brought round by a neighbour and deposited on my bed.

---

13 March/44

I run after my own tail, missing it! But I had meant, before now, to ease Your Excellency's mind at least; if not your heart—by telling you that you are not to worry your brain by trying to make it learn too much. If you have managed some, why, leave it at that and stop. And do not be distressed over not knowing them literally; if you err, why, in this at least err gaily, as and how may chance. I will promise not to hold you too strictly to account; I will kiss your hands for every alternate slip: now could any penalty be prettier?

It's not altogether astonishing you should be a little worn, considering all. And as I do not wish to treat you as the Prioress did Soeur Thérèse, I will have you go as gently as you will. You certainly will not read the *Prelude*[15]—for your sake and mine and the Divine Wordsworth's: and let the poems wait—until you come. If you are in London, and can, so do. You are not at all useless, even in bed; We could not suppose it. Sleep and rest for Us, and for me. How can We expect you to be ready?—how can you come to school?—unless you do. For if you are ever to say agreeably and charmingly that you have been a truant, why, must you not be debonair to say so? Prison was well for a week, but be released in mind from it now; pretend you do but linger on the road; if you find yourself late, why you can challenge me on it with a smile—yes? Or how can I be quite unfair to you if you will not play fair with me? So you must be as good as you can, in order that you may be treated scandalously; this is a very odd claim, but have with you! And as for taking too long a time, O well, we cannot have you so, and the rest you take from Us We will restore to you, making our profit from it on the way. Consider this at least as seriously as my sin. I will have a headache instead of you if it should so chance; might it not? You are very sweet and courteous, and the Holy Spirit shall heal you yet.

Ever,
C. W.

21 March/44

Let me first acknowledge the safe arrival of your book. I shall read it with the greatest interest; if any remarks occur to me I will make them, but what do I know of the way to talk to children? Be as Ourself among them—and much more satisfactorily! If anything can be done here, it shall be, but be quite at ease: I will not fidget. And thank you for sending it.

As for knowing how bad you are—why, I have but to look in my own glass! There is no monotony of—let us say, in general, *wrongness* which 'a

---

[15]This had been my next set-task.

man of my age' doesn't know. It may be one thing or another; whatever it is, and it's generally several; it is the equivalent of any. All the years? All the months? All the days? All to no better result? Well, but then, if there *had* been a better result, it would perhaps be more visible, even more useful, to others than to oneself; perhaps one cannot always suppose that even one's own judgement is the final, though indeed I agree one had better not envisage a perfection of which one isn't aware; and it's proper you should think as you do—your crown shall surprise you more than anyone!

Numerology is an ancient myth, and likely to have something to it. But I am very ill up in it. The pentagram is easier—it is a sign in some traditions of any occult Rite. Thus drawn the proper way which is—

Beginning here, you make it in that order, and that is for the Banishment of Evil Spirits or Elementals and the stabilizing of the good. But drawn reversed, which would be upside down and against the sun, it is the very opposite, and magically evil. Like all widdershins signs. And though these things have nothing to do with 'pure religion and undefiled', still I allow I should not care consciously and deliberately to draw a reversed pentagram, any more than I should care to say the Lord's prayer backwards or (like the Wicked Man in my new novel) try and pronounce the Reversed Tetragrammaton—if you know what that is. Do you know the Hebrew letters for it—

Yod;He;Vau;He

which are the Letters of the Divine Name that once a year before the Temple fell the High Priest pronounced in the Holy of Holies. Under the Shekinah. But (Blessed be He!) since it fell, we do not at all know the true pronunciation.

—I have read some of the book and think it very agreeable. I'm not sure how common human sacrifices once were, and I shouldn't myself be very certain about Nirvana and Buddhism being sad. But these are small points; the care and clarity are admirable. If I can do anything, I will, but my judgement (alas!) is not final here. As for intellect and intuition—no; I will discuss that another time.

As for Your Excellency's report—what should I say but that you are full of discretion and good care? You will be an example to me soon, and I shall grow very peevish. But honestly, Lalage, there is nothing to worry about. I do not believe you would have believed once you would do so delicately! (Just to satisfy both of us, you'll have three handsome stripes, against a chair, for inattention—but only that Your Handsomeness may be contented: yes?)

I had better post this, or it won't reach you this week.

In God,
C. W .

With the coming of spring my strength was beginning to return. I got up and went downstairs to lie on a rug in our little wilderness of a garden—and think. Mentally I was vividly alive: it was as if my illness had purged my mind, so that now I saw clearly how Charles had created a fantasy figure called Lalage who had never been Lois. I was back again with the question which had initiated our correspondence, back with my original "Jane." I had asked him in that first letter to define for me the object of love in the Dantean experience. Now I extended the question beyond that experience. Was there, I wondered, anything in Charles's feelings for his wife, for his Celia, for me, that had to do with us as persons in the actualities of our human state?

My mother and I were planning to leave Thaxted after Easter, with the object of eventually returning to Canterbury, although this would not be possible at once. I wrote to Charles and suggested a visit to Oxford early in May, by which time I hoped to be fully recovered, and the move accomplished.

6 April/44

I was going to write you a line for Easter, and the acknowledgement of the E.P.M.[16] may begin it.—You will—I will not say consider; perhaps that would be, for the moment, too rational a word; but you may properly be aware that a certain Risenness works in you; I will go farther and say that your You-ness is risen. I am very well aware that, whenever one is so aware, one immediately becomes so full of irritations, fantasies and glooms that it is quite remarkable, though not unnatural—being aware of the one, one is also more secretly aware of the other, and therefore more exposed. The mystery of the good and the not-good is very deeply knit; and if the Tree of Knowledge is close to the Tree of Life, why, the opposite is also true. So that, whether it is a question of that Life which shows to us in Joseph or Celia, or the more direct and devotional statement, it is still not surprising that we should find ourselves eating the wrong fruit on those very intermingled branches. Let us turn you a verse on it, and end so. But first—the poems any time; the first week in May (so far as I at present see) by all means; you will let me know your new address; and be ever blessed!

C. W.

Lalge said: 'Not indeed only
    that I stole the fruit, but (at that) of the wrong kind.
It is true (fact, not excuse) I was lonely
    among the trees, dim-eyed, oppressed in mind,
sick at heart; and the colour showed bright
    and ripe amid the leaves: so much for fact.
But here is the half-gnawed fruit—a revolting sight!'
    She tossed it angrily down, and in the act
it burst over the floor; she blushed. I said:
    'This, Lalage, is sheer snobbish pride;
blush? you deserve elsewhere to burn red,
    and shall now; but to-night, on each side,
coming to supper, a herald shall cry your name,
and the crown I set now on your brow flame.'

[16]His book, *The English Poetic Mind.*

For the first time, probably because I was still feeling weak, I allowed myself to be hurt by Charles's play of paradox. Crowns and heralds were all very well; but it seemed to me that I had had no opportunity, while I was ill, to commit any very heinous offence. I wrote back at once, anxiously inquiring if there had been a particular reason for his "gravity"; and was the more inclined to suppose that there had been when he did not reply to my letter for three weeks.

---

27 April/44

Condescend, most excellent Theophila—I wonder if St. Luke really had anyone special in mind, and if the word was but a cover, like Lycidas or Adonais. Or indeed Celia, though I take it not Joseph—well, condescend to attribute to the cares and labours of this world an apparent discourtesy of delay. Term has been beginning, and lectures and tutorials, and all the oddments continue, and I . . . though this indeed is almost excuse, and I concede to you what small penalty you will . . or I will pay my courtesies when you come. Time is the dungeon of my intentions, yet I know, as Bunyan did, that I carry the key in my breast; the key is perhaps the 'white bird' of the other saying.

Thursday, 11th May, if that suits you, by all means. I will meet you as before. But you asked me a question I haven't answered. And as for writing 'gravely'—it must have been the weather or the war or some accidental otherness of imagination. It makes my own delay the more grievous—excuse again. No, indeed: I think you are—all considered—remarkably perseverent in good: your 'general badness' is shot everyway with virtue, and you keep truth with truth. O if you linger on a warm afternoon, or sleep under a side-hedge when you should be . . studying geometry, God 'ild you, anything done about it is between two smiles. There was a pleasant phrase in *Seed of Adam* which fits you, and which you may write out a dozen times—'tis but two words—and give me before you repeat as much as you have of Milton—'Light's lazybones'. But O if none of us had more to bewail!

Ever,
C. W.

I travelled to Oxford knowing that I must oppose Charles
in two stages. First I must demand an answer to my original question. This in itself would be a challenge to the
whole intellectual structure on which he based his life,
and would lead up to what I must then do, which was
simply to tell him that I could not go on. I could not continue our relationship on the terms he had laid down for
it. I knew that I must do this, if necessary, at the cost of
losing Charles; but I told myself that, of course, this need
not—would not—be the case. After all that had been between us, we were surely and forever—friends. And yet I
was horribly afraid. I knew very well how deep would be
his chagrin and disappointment.

The first stage of my rebellion was enacted over lunch.
I demanded a defence of the Dantean way of love against
the charge of being impersonal, inhuman, unconcerned with
the actuality of its supposed object. (Although I did not
entirely realise this at the time, I was not being so bold as
to challenge the validity of the *Vita Nuova* itself, still less
of the great edifice of poetry and theology finally constructed by Dante on the basis of his love. All this had
meant a great deal to me in the past, and would again. What
I was immediately concerned with was the way in which
Charles was applying his own interpretation of Dante to
his own and other people's experience.) To my amazement,
Charles declared, almost casually, that of course I was
perfectly right. He admitted the charge. I was silenced. I
can only explain his reaction by recalling that there was in
Charles a burning intensity of honesty that would often
result in his seizing upon that side of a paradox that he
was personally disposed to reject, and emphasising it—
momentarily at least—for the purpose of reminding himself of his own fallibility and the possibility of his having
fallen short of the truth. Later, he would return to the
very same position he had occupied before: there is this
advantage in turning every question into an absolute paradox, that meaning tends to disappear between the opposites, relieving one of the necessity for commitment.

All the same, I could see that he was very much perturbed. Towards the end of the meal, he asked me what, if the Dantean way of love seemed to me so inadequate, I would suggest that Dante might have put in its place.

"Why," I said, "a human relationship."

The answer seemed to me obvious to the point of foolishness. But Charles's response to it was to gaze at me with that wounding intentness that was like nothing else that I have ever experienced, and then ask:

"But child, what if his humanity were not human? How then could he have a human relationship?"

And again I remembered the cry of Taliessin in his grief:

'It is a doubt if my body is flesh or fish . . .
            hapless the woman who loves me . . .'

We went on to Southfield House. In his office I began to tell him that I could not continue my "obedience." I was not allowed even to finish what I was trying to say. Springing to his feet and pacing the room, he declared that, of course, naturally, I must be loosed at once. No questions, no reproaches, simply acquiescence. Quickly he took a small book, seemingly at random, from a shelf and presented it to me as a keepsake. (It was called *Christian Symbolism* and was under Michal's name; though Charles murmured, as he handed it to me, that most of it had been written by him.) Then he showed me to the door, bowed, kissed my hand with great tenderness, and adjured me: "Go with God." I went. It was as if some vital part of me had been suddenly and mercilessly torn out; and the fact that I had done this to myself made the resulting laceration all the harder to accept. In the streets of the city I wept into a pocket handkerchief.

After that, I heard nothing for three months. When I did eventually get a letter, I felt that in view of the facts, which were that I had given him an address before leaving Thaxted and had written to him several times since, and he now had three addresses any one of which would have found me, his lame excuses made but little sense.

---

31 Aug/44

The absurdest thing happened, or I should have written, I hope, long since. I had put your letters together, and before I went to London I put away all my private correspondence. Yes—but when I came back, I discovered your earlier Guildford letters[17] weren't with the later, and could I find them among my stuff? all the, as one might say, more personal and private—yes, but *not* the original Guildford address. They are there—or it is there—certainly, and I should have found it, in time. But I apologise, I genuflect, and I am much relieved that you wrote.

I am sending back the book—which (the return of it, I mean) disappoints and annoys me. I had hoped we should do it. The trouble is that, though we all liked it, we haven't any series or anything it would fit into. Or so—and I think truly—the Juvenile Department protest. You may well say that if I like it, and everyone likes it, why do we demur? To which I can only say that that's the difficulty with us; we are so laden with books that a sort of unattached thing of this length and size tends to fall unnoticed. But you will not think that it returns 'unwept, unhonoured, and unsung'; well, unsung perhaps, but not the others! (And where does that quotation come from?)

I am, in fact, that apart, much relieved to be writing this. I could not avoid a slight fear that you might have supposed, faintly, that our general decision last time was resulting in an entire lack of concern. Which is no more true than it would have been decorous. And I hope all goes well. I rather congratulate you on your nursery school; you ought to be very good at it. And I hope that, in reason, you practise a charming 'holy indifference'. Shakespeare defined our proper limits when he wrote 'no more than with a pure blush thou mayst come off withal'.

All blessings. The MS. goes to you by registered post to-day. And forgive me everything.

Ever,
C. W.

---

[17]My first three letters had been written from a Guildford address, to which I had temporarily returned in the early summer of 1944.

Impetuously and no doubt unwisely, I sat down at once and wrote a long unhappy letter, protesting that, whatever Charles might say, it was clear that I had only mattered to him as the slave girl in his myth. This accusation went unanswered. Some weeks later I came across a review of C. S. Lewis which Charles had lent me and I had forgotten to return. It was not important, I doubted if he had thought about it since; but I sent it back.

Southfield House
10 Oct/44

I have been, whatever you might think, delaying in order to send you a copy of the new poems.[18] Which we succeed in getting off to-day, I hope. And I also hope that any views you may have held about my limitations to—shall we say?—'slaves' may be dispelled, and that the poems, as well as I, may be free. I should—egotistically, much less in a lordlier sense—hate to have them spoiled for you. If one may discreetly say so.

It was sweet of you to return CSL. I'd quite forgotten you'd got it. And I hope the job—and you—do well. Let me hear how all goes. Term is opening here, and I plunge into lectures and tutorials; and a maddening lot of incidentals, reviews, and odd addresses and so on. Reputation, my dear Lalage, is, I now find, largely a matter of doing things you don't want to do for people you don't want to see. 'Have courage, my boy, to say No.' Yes, but ought one? Well, ascribed—and so forth.

Anyhow, forgive me and admire me. You've seen all the poems, but they look better in a book. Besides, it will show you I am not in fact myself the slave of one pattern—no; all right: do not throw a plate at me.

In God,
C. W.

---

[18]*The Region of the Summer Stars.*

In December I wrote to Charles with the news that I was receiving instruction at Westminster Cathedral, and was about to become a Roman Catholic. I mentioned that my brother too had been drawn to the Church of Rome and, had he lived, would almost certainly have become a priest.

Southfield House
14 Dec/44

All blessings! . . Well, and so again. What else could I—should I?—say? Be ever blessed and ever fortunate. The City, it seems, expands, one way and another, round you: in experience, I mean, and you as a growing citizen. All the Peace with you always.

It's odd about your brother. Certainly you seem to live a double life. You are a good girl, Lalage, and I expect you to be even more than good in the end. It was sweet of you to let me know.

Here nothing unusual happens. I clear off oddments before beginning the prose book on Arthur and the High Prince. We have sold out, it seems, the first edition of the *Summer Stars*. The novel is expected early in the New Year.

Every kind of benediction—at Christmas and beyond!

C. W.

For Christmas I sent Charles a silver crucifix, copied from an antique model, which I had found in an antique shop.

21 Dec/44

How very kind of you! I shall keep it with the greatest care . . with some reference to the Divine Beatrice and to all who have learned something from that kind of Way, whether by the following of it or the being taken from it. Did I ever tell you that the Mother Superior of the Roman Convent of the Sacred Heart here at Oxford had a particular feeling for the

Figure of Beatrice? It seems her own Way began with a twenty minutes' chat at a dance with a young man she never saw again!

All Blessings!
C. W.

At this time I was living temporarily in Hampstead, not realising (for I had never known in what part of London he lived) that I was barely ten minutes' walk from Charles's home. It was therefore not surprising that I had a chance encounter with him on an Underground train. I was travelling with the same cousin who had known him at Downe House; and it was she who caught sight of him first. Catching my arm, she exclaimed: "Isn't that Charles Williams?" Charles was standing at the other end of the compartment, near the doors, studying a sheaf of manuscript.

Terrified as I was of receiving further evidence of his indifference, I lurched towards him down the train. Touching him on the arm, I said: "Hullo"; and was instantly conscious of a wild inappropriateness in the situation, and in the lame little word which was all that I felt able to bring out. Charles gave a violent start and blushed literally to the roots of his hair. Then he grasped my hand with a warmth that was altogether unassumed, said something which I scarcely understood and afterwards could not remember, so overcome was I by the shock of the moment—and was gone. The doors had opened; and, whether or not we had arrived at his intended destination, Charles had got out. "My goodness," was Margery's comment, "how he blushed. I never saw a man blush so in my life."

For the time being, I abandoned the idea of becoming a Roman Catholic. Joseph had announced his engagement. I felt a great desire to talk to Charles about these two crucial happenings in my life; and so I wrote to him again. It appears from his reply that I suggested the possibility of meeting in London to save myself expense: certainly I was very hard up; but my recollection is that I was an-

gling for an invitation to his home. It was not until after
his death that I came to understand how firmly and completely Charles had separated his family from his friends.
(This may well have been a great mistake. Michal was a
sociable woman who enjoyed being hospitable and bitterly
resented being overlooked. When eventually I came to
know her well, I realised that her obsessive jealousy was
not of Charles's friends: she disliked them in general, for
no other reason than that she suspected Charles of seeing
Phillida in their company. Had he felt able to invite
people to the house in the normal way, this would almost
certainly have allayed her suspicions and eased the ten-
sions of their relationship. In fact, towards the end of his
life, he was not seeing Phillida very often: his terror of
provoking Michal, born no doubt of past tempests,
prompted him to a deviousness that was unnecessary and
must have had the opposite effect from the one he intended. But Charles was incapable of behaving naturally
in any context.)

Southfield House
18 Jan./45

(I've been away to speak at Birmingham which is why I didn't answer
at once.)

The names were in the *Telegraph:* I saw them by pure chance after
your letter had come. Well . . it is the second step, so to speak. I do not
even now sit quite easily to the awareness of the husband of the Lady of the
Window—though I don't dislike him . . . and I am a little conscious that at
least, by now, I am not wholly sorry to be free of exterior responsibility.
The interior responsibility of willing their entire felicity . . ? m'm. All but
entire—is what I feel would suit me better; a little regret in her, a little
yearning, a little (the very tiniest) jealousy in her of others still . . something like that would still placate me . . Ass!

This is not, I hope, as irrelevant as it sounds. As for you and me—
you said nothing wrong; be at ease. London is difficult because the times
are so short; and because the only way of making marriage through these
years is to keep these times for it. But you will let the least of your
servants say that there is no reason why we shouldn't, say, split the ex-

pense. And though we have got it clear that you are no mythical slave or anything, there are still times when it would be proper for you to be merely obedient?

It looks, now Term is beginning, as if Fridays were my best day. Monday is sometimes London; Tuesday I have a lecture; Wednesday a tutorial; Thursday I keep in case—never mind. Would some Friday suit you?

Always,
C. W.

I must have suggested a date and time for our meeting. His note confirming this is missing: presumably I destroyed it as being of no interest. I went to Oxford and met Charles at the Randolph. We lunched, but not at our usual corner table (I wondered if this was coincidence; or if, which would have been typical of Charles, that table had for him some particular and semi-ritual significance). Afterwards we sat in the lounge. Nothing was as it had been before (had I supposed that it could be?—yes, I had prayed for a "middle way," some trace at least of his former tenderness and warmth); until at the very end, when it was time for him to go, he swept me into the centre of the lounge and there, as if we were on a stage and the startled guests of the Randolph were the audience, bent down, with that queer twist and flourish that was entirely peculiar to himself, and kissed my hand.

Three months later he was dead.

Michal's choice for the gravestone was perfect. But I have my own epitaph for him, which comes from his poem *The Calling of Taliessin,* where the king's poet sings of his mysterious lineage, of how he was "tangled . . . by the hazel bush" and "mangled for a night and a day by black swine":

> *yet my true region is the summer stars.*

Feast of the Annunciation. 1985

✑*Notes*

by Glen Cavaliero

Page	Line	
15	1	Charles Williams is buried in the graveyard of St. Cross Church, Holywell, in St. Cross Road.
16	19	George MacDonald (1824–1905) Scottish novelist, theologian and poet. *Phantastes* (1858) and *Lilith* (1895) are fantasies written for adults. The latter clearly influenced Williams' novel *Descent into Hell* (1937).
19	7	The Order of the Golden Dawn was founded in 1888 by S. L. MacGregor Mathers, William Wynn Westcott, and W. R. Woodman.
21	18	Downe House was founded by Olive Willis in 1907. It was originally housed in Charles Darwin's old home in Kent.
21	24	Myra Hess (1880–1965) became renowned for her heroic organisation of concerts held in the National Gallery during the London blitz.
21	26	*A Myth of Bacon* was performed at the school in 1932. It was published in the Charles Williams Society Newsletter, nos. 11, 12, and 14.
22	39	*The Three Temptations* was included in Charles Williams' *Collected Plays*, published in 1963 with an Introduction by John Heath-Stubbs.
26	29	The reference is to "The Redeemed City," included in *The Image of the City* (1958), 102–10.
27	1	St. Thomas Aquinas' quotation comes from Boethius' *The Consolations of Philosophy*, book 5, sect. 6.
33	11	The quotation is from "The Calling of Taliessin" in *The Region of the Summer Stars*, 14.
35	11	In the midst of the word he was trying to say, In the midst of his laughter and glee, He had softly and suddenly vanished away— For the Snark *was* a Boojum, you see. (Lewis Carroll, *The Hunting of the Snark*)
36	6	In Williams' novel *Descent into Hell*, Pauline Anstruther is haunted by the Doppelgänger or replica of herself. Initially an experience of dread, it is transformed through her growth in love and obedience into a vision of her true and glorious state as held in the mind of God.

Page	Line	
39	6	Williams refers to the sonnet in the second chapter of *The Figure of Beatrice* (1943), 24.
41	25	"Catch as catch can; but absence is a catch of the presence." "Palomides Before his Christening," *Taliessin Through Logres*, 67.
41	29	The Skeleton or *Figura Rerum* (appearance of things) is an embodiment of the chastening providence of God which reveals Cranmer's true nature to himself and thus impels him towards salvation.
43	3	Palomides, in Williams' version of the Arthuriad, is a follower of Islam, who is converted to Christianity through loss of romantic vision and the bankruptcy of his desires.
43	17	"Celsitude": obsolescent term meaning exalted character, high rank, lofty position.
43	34	"Amicitia": friendship.
44	14	Coventry Patmore (1823–96), poet and theologian of romantic love. His long poem *The Angel in the House* (1854–62) was a major influence on Williams' early poetry. His prose work *The Rod, the Root, and the Flower* (1895) contains much that was to be developed in the latter's theology of romantic love.
46	20	Sephirotic tradition: In her Introduction to *The Image of the City* Anne Ridler emphasises (xxiv) the great importance for Williams' thought of his study of A. E. Waite's *The Secret Doctrine in Israel* (1913), an exposition of the Jewish Cabbala, in which the symbolism of the Sephirotic Tree, or Tree of Life, is systematically expounded.
49	28	P'o-l'u: Williams varied his spelling of this word. It is also written in this manner in his late play *The House of the Octopus;* in *Taliessin through Logres* it is spelled P'o-lu.
51	6	The quotation is from the *Summa Theologica*, part 3, 45.
51	20	John Duns Scotus (c. 1270–1308) influenced Williams through his teaching that the Incarnation would have happened even had there been no Fall. For Williams' discussion of this theme, see his essay "Natural Goodness" in *The Image of the City*, 75–80.
53	6	"Still were I thrall to Lalage's sweet laughter And sweeter speech." (Horace, Ode 22 [trans. Edward Marsh])
53	19	" . . . in the deep nook, where once Thou call'dst me up at midnight to fetch dew From the still-vex'd Bermoothes. . . ." (*The Tempest*, act 1, sc. 2, lines 227–29)
53	32	"Alice Mary" was Alice Mary Hennell, later Hadfield, subsequently Williams' biographer.
55	11	Eliot's "Dante" is to be found in his *Selected Essays* (1932).
55	30	Williams edited *The Letters of Evelyn Underhill* (1943) for which he provided a lengthy Introduction.
56	8	Shekinah: Cabbalistic term signifying the manifestation of the Glory of God dwelling among men.
60	22	Dorothy Leigh Sayers (1893–1957), detective story writer, Dante scholar, and theologian.
64	14	*The New Christian Year*, an anthology of readings from Christian writers, was published in 1941.

Page	Line	
64	19	St. Seraphim of Sarov (1759–1833), Russian monk and spiritual teacher. Williams quotes from him a number of times in *The New Christian Year.*
65	4	"Keep thy conscience. . . . " The passage is in *The New Christian Year,* 147.
66	3	C. S. Lewis' *The Allegory of Love: A Study in Medieval Tradition* was published in 1936. Its treatment of the theology of Romantic Love led to Williams' friendship with the author.
67	5	The comment on Shakespeare will be found in *The Forgiveness of Sins* (1942), 175.
71	4	This edition of Athanasius' *De Incarnatione* was almost certainly the one translated by a Religious of C.S.M.V. with an Introduction by C. S. Lewis, published in 1944.
71	10	*proporia motu:* of her own accord.
73	31	Under the pseudonym "Elizabeth," Mary Annette Beauchamp (1866–1941) published eighteen novels between 1898 and 1941. They are characterised by high spirits and a keen sense of the ridiculous.
74	6	Soeur Thérèse: St. Thérèse of Lisieux (1873–97) author of *The Diary of a Soul.*
78	12	"Lycidas": pseudonym for Edward King in Milton's poem of that name. "Adonais": pseudonym for John Keats in the elegy on him by Shelley.
78	19	The Bunyan reference is to Christian's discovery of the Key of Promise while in the dungeon of Giant Despair, as recounted in part one of *The Pilgrim's Progress.*
78	32	"Light's lazybones": see *Collected Plays,* 152.
80	23	*Christian Symbolism:* "I wrote Christian Symbolism years ago (with Charles 99% assistance). Charles uncle ran something called The Talbot Press & I did it for him." Michal Williams to Glen Cavaliero, 18 July 1956.
81	17	The wretch, concentred all on self,

<blockquote>
The wretch, concentred all on self,
Living, shall forfeit fair renown,
And, doubly dying, shall go down
To the vile dust, from whence he sprung,
Unwept, unhonoured and unsung.
    (Sir Walter Scott,
      The Lay of the Last Minstrel, canto 6, stanza 13)
</blockquote>

Page	Line	
81	26	Williams is presumably (mis)quoting Shakespeare's Celia. ". . . love no man in good earnest; nor no further in sport neither, than with safety of a pure blush thou mayst in honour come off again."

<blockquote>
(*As You Like It,* act 1, sc. 2, lines 27–29)
</blockquote>